SUNSETS AND DOGSHITS

SUNSETS AND DOGSHITS

Sean Ashton

ALMA BOOKS

ALMA BOOKS LTD
London House
243–253 Lower Mortlake Road
Richmond
Surrey TW9 2LL
United Kingdom
www.almabooks.com

Sunsets and Dogshits first published by Alma Books Limited in 2007
Copyright © Sean Ashton, 2007

This is a work of fiction. Names, characters, places and incidents either are
the product of the author's imagination or are used fictitiously, and any
resemblance to actual persons, living or dead, business establishments,
events or locales is entirely coincidental.

Printed in Jordan by National Press

ISBN-13 (HARDBACK): 978-1-84688-045-2
ISBN-10 (HARDBACK): 1-84688-045-9

Contents

To my parents

It's not where you start, it's where you finish.

Luckey Davis

SUNSETS AND DOGSHITS

The 2006 World Mincing Championships

Enthusiasts and trivia buffs will know that mincing, like so many sports, was invented pretty much by accident. The first *recorded* mince was executed by Captain William Tobias Glover when he squeaked down the gangplank of the HMS *Japonica* in May 1906, his buttocks clenched tightly together to stave off a severe case of the runs that had ambushed his constitution during the short walk from the bridge to midship. Unable either to go back – a bottleneck of ranking officers ruled out that option – or break into a full sprint for the nearest dockside convenience, for fear of losing face in front of the huge Warwick Island crowd that had gathered to welcome the ship alongside, the unfortunate Captain had to stifle his motion until he had shaken not only the Chief Administrator's hand, but that of every dignitary, councillor, magistrate, policeman and blacksmith that had been convened into an official welcoming committee. Legend has it (though the Pathé footage does not corroborate this) that the Captain, before darting into a shipping crate to relieve himself, had also to stand motionless, perspiration beading his inscrutable brow, while a brass section of lobster fishermen discharged a flatulent rendition of 'God Save the King'.

But it was not this alone – I mean the Captain's cloacal plight – that spawned a pastime. Had he not turned to his Commander and bade him, "Walk as I do, walk as I do, man," and had not the latter assumed the Captain was adopting a custom designed to endear the crew to the inhabitants of this diminutive British dependency – had *not* that gentleman, together with the Lieutenant Commander, Lieutenant, Sub-Lieutenant, Midshipman and every other debarking seaman, mimicked the Captain's gait, it might well have been construed as a mere orthopaedic anomaly, or as the symptom of an injury sustained in some distant naval conflict. Instead, history was made. For the fact that the *entire* crew sashayed onto dry land like a troop of raving madams not only disguised the Captain's impediment as a new development in naval ceremony, but inspired the islanders – many of whom were relatively new settlers anxious to dispel the rumour that expatriation had dulled their gentlemanly instincts – to adopt, thereafter, precisely the same fastidious bearing in their respective milieux.

To call the first faltering minces that graced these remote South Pacific salons a full-blown sporting phenomenon would be an exaggeration. But they *were* a decisive beginning, if only because the trappings associated with its initial adoption as a pre-prandial parlour game – costume jewellery, cummerbunds, the ambulatory consumption of crème de menthe – are all still very much a part of mincing. In fact, its growth as a sport was built on, and continues to be sustained

– 4 –

by, the exclusive sponsorship of couturiers and aperitif manufacturers. (The sport was amateur until 1968, but from as early as 1952 the top mincers were making twice as much money from endorsements as from their day jobs.)

The man credited with introducing the first rules was Sir Adam Deuchars IV, Chief Administrator of Warwick when the *Japonica* made landfall there in 1906. Historians will recall that it was Deuchars's great-grandfather, Adam Robert Deuchars, who had first lobbied for the colonization of Warwick in 1831, but not until Victoria ascended the throne in 1837 was full permission given to secure the uninhabited monticule.

Deuchars the Elder's original mandate to govern has since passed to successive generations, the most recent incumbent being the 2006 World Mincing Championships' Tournament Director (and long-time advisor to the WMO), James Reginald Deuchars. I was lucky enough to meet James Reginald at the reception given after Sunday's opening ceremony. In fact, I'll come clean and admit that it was during this interview that I gleaned most of what I have already told you about mincing. I was especially fascinated to learn that the man most regularly cited as the godfather of the sport is, thankfully, neither the hapless Captain Glover nor the punctilious, rulebook-waving Adam Deuchars IV. According to James Reginald (as genealogically distant from Deuchars IV as Deuchars IV was from Deuchars the Elder), the man responsible for liberating the sport from the parlours of the bourgeoisie, the man who, in James Reginald's own words, first "picked up the ball and ran with it" is one Nathaniel Jepson. In 1913 Jepson was forced to winter on Warwick after his whaling vessel, the *Accentor*, had foundered on a reef to the south of the island. Quickly assimilated into the various cliques, salons and at-homes that constituted Warwickian Society, Jepson surprised everyone by displaying none of the truculence that tended, in the eyes of his hosts, to afflict the captains of whaling vessels. On the contrary, Jepson was effusive and open. And he was not merely a tonic to mincing: he was indeed, as James Reginald suggests, its William Webb Ellis.

The decisive moment, explained James Reginald, occurred on Jepson's society debut, at a dinner given by the Chief Administrator. Jepson had arrived early and had been standing sheepishly on his own, some distance from the Deucharses' front gate, waiting in vain for any of the few people whose acquaintance he had been able to make in his short time on the island. Seeing no such person, he eventually took the plunge, striding purposefully up to the porch, only to be stopped at the threshold. "Excuse me sir," said the butler, handing Jepson a small mahogany disc and ushering him inside. "If sir *wouldn't* mind waiting here till *his* turn... I presume sir *will* be mincing tonight?..." Before Jepson could proffer his outsider's bafflement, the butler had wheeled round to attend to some even later arrivals. The porch was crowded and oppressive, and all the guests seemed to be men. Beyond this crammed vestibule lay a vast hall, the threshold to which was guarded by a second butler who was calling out numbers. Every so often a guest moved forwards and took his place behind a scarlet rope with a brass hook at one end. Announcing the gentleman's name, the butler unhooked the rope, and the guest waltzed double-time into the space beyond, his cute quick steps percussing the floor with an ungulate clatter, shiny leather boots squeaking like rodents. Halfway across, he attempted a pirouette – and narrowly avoided falling, as his wooden hoof skated over the marble. No sooner had he made it to the other side of the hall – gathered into the arms of a female welcoming committee that filled the doorway to the dining room – than another performer was summoned to the rope. Dressed in raiment of impossible gaiety, this gentleman had a somewhat different technique, his legs and hips rotating in such freelance fashion they seemed to be attempting to escape his torso. Nevertheless, the torso followed gamely, with the head in hot pursuit, and the old fruit was borne obliquely across the parlour with the precarious rapidity of an amateur unicyclist, careering past the ladies and collapsing directly into his seat at the dining table.

It was at this point that Jepson recalled the words the butler had spoken – "I presume sir *will* be mincing tonight?…" – and suddenly felt the disc in his hand, which he noticed bore the number 18. Number 16 had just been called; there was still time to make it outside before his own number was called… what, and risk certain ostracism from the most influential community on the island? Offend no less a figure than the Chief Administrator himself? It would be imprudent to begin social relations thus. His arrival on Warwick had been inauspicious enough: he was known only as a captain who had lost his ship. It was as well for him that non-seafaring people have not the faintest idea of the humiliation entailed in such a loss – which is so mortifying that many captains prefer to go down with their vessels. But these thoughts (which had consumed what little time there still was to make a discreet exit) were dispersed by riotous applause as another guest, number 17, shuffled across the parlour, elbows jammed into his ribcage, arms flailing limply. Number 17 was gathered into the dining room by a roseate dowager, and Jepson now found himself bustled towards the rope. The butler, who appeared at a distance an imposing sentinel, at closer quarters proved an eager and sympathetic squire: "Drink this, sir. Now, just keep your head up, focus on the dado rail and keep it simple." Knocking back the sherry that had been thrust into his hand, Jepson improvised a token warm-up routine, windmilling his arms and hyperventilating like a shackled escapologist about to be lowered into a water tank, before launching himself – and the hyperbole is quite warranted – into the unknown.

It would be no exaggeration to say that all the anxieties of the previous months – dwindling oil yields, the increasing disquiet of his crew, the catastrophic loss of the *Accentor* – were released in a single explosive catharsis. And yet the actual manœuvre, the specific biomechanical convulsions that Nathaniel Jepson's body produced that evening, are probably less important than the distance it travelled. On approaching the doors to the dining room, Jepson took one look at the swaying anemone of eligible spinsters and thought, "I'm not going in *there*," and so the rookie's tour of duty was extended to include, first, a brief appraisal of the decor, and secondly (and most crucially), a *return to the rope* – which was interpreted as a direct challenge by another gentleman who was just moving into position. What followed, then, was the first *competitive* mince.

And the name of Jepson's opponent? Now, it is often the case that history sidelines its supporting cast, that posterity, having fixated so intently on the triumph of the *victor ludorum*, immediately forgets the name of the beaten finalist. But not in this instance. For Jepson's opponent that evening was none other than the Chief Administrator himself, who, gazing upon this preternaturally freestyle performance and realizing that his rulebook had either to be stoutly defended or else torn up, had crept round to the front of the house and demanded the next mince.

Jepson's other vital contribution, it will have been noted, was the introduction of the "return mince". There were of course other refinements he introduced that evening (another being the holding of the breath, borrowed from the Indian sport of kabaddi), but these were to prove the most significant. From this point on, no longer would mincing be restricted to a single leg undertaken by guests arriving at the front door and moving through the parlour to the dining room: the "return leg" challenged the notion that mincing was merely an ostentatious way of moving from one place to another. Mincing was no longer something a luncheon guest did on arrival out of etiquette; it became an activity in itself. Henceforth, mincers began to meet at *all* times of the day, regardless of whether any actual luncheon, tea or dinner was served. Jepson's debut had been the catalyst for transforming a frivolous social convention into a serious pastime. With the impetus of competition, mincing soon spread to the surrounding South Pacific dependencies and beyond, to Tierra del Fuego in the east and Christchurch in the south-west. Like cricket, it flourished in the British colonies, particularly in Burma and Singapore. By 1923 no less a figure than Baron Pierre de Coubertin, the first president of the IOC, was beginning to talk openly about mincing as a *sport* – though incredibly, not until 1946 did its most accomplished practitioners (typically, resting actors, maître d's and colonial adjutants whiling away the last hours of Empire) first come together and agree on the standardizations that have served it to this day.

Most sports, rather than being conceived "whole", tend to originate as an idle and disinterested tampering with reality. Golf, for example, was reputedly invented when one shepherd turned to another and wagered he could hit a pebble into a rabbit burrow in so many shots. According to Judith Frow, a sport is born when such activities "slip their quotidian moorings and are pursued entirely for their own inherent qualities… This autonomy is consolidated by the 'arena', 'pitch' or 'field of play', which reinforces the activity's detachment from everyday reality." We need hardly add that any crowd that happens to gather around this field of play further consolidates this autonomy by quite literally turning its back on everyday reality. In the spring of 1913, Nathaniel Jepson turned *his* back on the reality – the whaling reality – he had known since youth, choosing not to seek a passage back to England but to remain on Warwick and oversee the construction of mincing's first purpose-built arena. And yes, he found love there too, but that is another story.

It is on the site of this old building that the 2006 Championships are being staged. The tournament began with an upset, the unseeded Didier Le Faye (SUI) beating the highly fancied Justin Merrington (USA) in a match that went to a tiebreak after the score was locked at 4–4 in the final set. Given the relative dullness of the 2002 finals (when the WMO was rightly lambasted for allowing pay-per-view economics to influence its seeding), this result was just the tonic these championships needed, even if the match was a little untidy. Both men's technique buckled under pressure at different stages, and Merrington did not seem to have shaken off the hip problem that saw him pull out of the Bangkok Masters in April. If the WMO has got the seeding right this time, then Le Faye – assuming he defeats the Bulgarian qualifier Miroslav Zorekov in his last group match – will almost certainly meet reigning champion Peter Direction (ENG) in the next round, a big ask for the Swiss number four. Other results went with form, though events were not without their drama. Dominic Thorburn (NZL) beat Eugene McCulloch (NIR) 5–2 in an intriguing encounter that saw both men complain about the new synthetic surface, which apparently offered insufficient traction compared to the asphalt strip used in the qualifiers. McCulloch took the opening set and was three minces up in the second before his opponent, swapping his Jeffery-West Chelsea boots for a pair of rubber-soled Agnès B loafers, and donning a fresh Comme des Garçon dress shirt dripping with Cinzano endorsements, unleashed a typically flamboyant rearguard action. The Kent-based Ulsterman could find no reply, rallying briefly to take the sixth set before losing the final one to love.

Meanwhile, in Pool C the TK Maxx-sponsored Cuthbert Ladywell (ENG) won a tight and rather catty encounter with naturalized compatriot Jesse Fairfax. There's no love lost between these two mincers, and at one point the umpires literally had to separate them, Ladywell having veered into his opponent's lane. (The mince was rerun.) The match was an hour and twenty-one minutes old when the veteran and former antiquarian bookseller eventually prevailed 5–4, though I understand Fairfax's camp has lodged an appeal with the match officials. (The result is likely to stand; the last time the WMO overturned one was in 1982, when the East German Jörn Kelling was expelled from the competition for using banned stimulants.) The other Pool C match, an all-African affair between Asmerom

Muluneh (ERI) and Gus Pandy (ZIM), resumes this morning, with the Eritrean needing just one more set to complete a whitewash. The match began farcically for the Zimbabwean, who split his Farahs in the opening mince (an incident bound to feature in the light-hearted montage sequence the BBC will undoubtedly put together as an epitaph to these finals), and quickly got worse as he defaulted the return leg for "lifting". From that point it was downhill all the way. In Pool D, László Jankowiak (POL) blew hot and cold in his match against Álvaro Álvarez (MEX), but was eventually blown away 5–3 by the fiery Mexican. Janko's reputation is built largely on his stamina and resolve, but on this occasion when the going got tough, the tough just never seemed quite able to get going. At thirty-seven, that is surely the last we will see of the celebrated Pole on the world stage, though there is always the senior tour – an increasingly lucrative option for mincers of Janko's profile. Elsewhere, the young Sri Lankan Roshan Rwegasira won his second Pool E match against Elquemedo Herrero of Cuba by default after his opponent suffered a recurrence of the knee-ligament injury sustained in February's epic French Open encounter with Peter Direction. The Negombo-based student, representing his country for the first time in a World Championship, now faces 1998 semi-finalist Jefferson James Cassidy III (USA) in what is effectively a mince-off for a place in the knockout stages (Herrero having withdrawn from the tournament and Direction having already qualified). The American will have

– 13 –

to improve on his performance in the last meeting between these two mincers, when he only just edged out the inexperienced Sri Lankan 5–4.

The best match of the group stage so far – Le Faye's triumph notwithstanding – has to be the Pool F encounter between Paolo Carlino (ITA) and Valerie Fotheringale (ENG). Both men needed one more win to guarantee qualification for the knockout stage, and both were at the top of their game. Although Fotheringale raced to a two-set lead, the Italian ran out a 5–2 winner. But the match was much closer than the score suggests, Carlino having won all five of his sets by just a single mince, and Fotheringale having won both of his to love. The recent change in the scoring system – each set is now *first to* rather than *best of* five minces – definitely suits Carlino's attritional temperament. In each of the last three sets Fotheringale took a 3–0 lead, only to lose 5–4. He would have flourished in an earlier era, when there was a break between the end of the outward and the beginning of the return mince, and when style and deportment were favoured over speed and endurance. A knowledgeable crowd clearly thought the Sicilian was rushing the Brit on the return leg, but the reigning Commonwealth Champion – who has been training at altitude in a bid to attain full fitness – was quick to scotch any suggestions of gamesmanship: "I'm aware that in the past Paolo has used every possible advantage to win matches, but I'd just like to say that today I thought he minced fantastically well, and within the rules. His hip rotation was a little out of sync in the early sets, and I thought I did well to take full advantage of that, but fair play to the guy: he just hangs in there and won't let go. He always gives one hundred and ten percent. He's a credit to mincing." Carlino was equally generous to his opponent: "In Italy, Valerie is a big mincing icon. As a boy I studied his technique. For me to defeat him is the proudest day of my life." And all is not lost for Fotheringale; for, having won the most individual minces of the current third-placed group members, he stands an excellent chance of qualifying through the repêchage. Neutrals would relish a rematch between these two mincers, who left the arena to a standing ovation and shouts of "Minced Valerie! Minced Paolo!". Should both players advance to the knockout stages, they cannot meet again until the final. Stranger things have happened.

As usual I've gone on for too long, but it would be criminal to sign off without mentioning the exemplary TV coverage of these championships. Desmond Kelleher, a useful county mincer in his day, is anchoring for ITV, while the BBC have given Dougie Donelly the chance to add yet another feather to his presentational cap. Dougie's appetite for sporting confrontation of all kinds is insatiable, and in this author's opinion worthy of an OBE.

– *The Montrose Observer*, 2006

Twats, Cunts and Arseholes
of England and Wales

Opinion is divided as to the intention and merit of Stuart Kilcline's most recent work. Executed in exactly the same format as earlier pieces – as a poster "issued" by a factitious institution – *Twats, Cunts and Arseholes of England and Wales* dares us to revise our judgement of *Recent Posters*, the ongoing series from which it is the latest offering. In such works as *Bollards and Posts of Greater London*, *Holes and Orifices of Great Britain and Ireland* and *Arboreal Disfigurement: Scars, Lesions and Tumescence*, the photographer – so we thought – laid his cards squarely on the table, presenting himself as the affable custodian of left-field taxonomies. But perhaps the warning signs were there in *Stuff Chucked Mindlessly into Trees and Bushes* and *Sunsets and Dogshits*, a prognosis this latest piece would seem to confirm, appearing as it does to renounce the benign spirit of earlier works, which focused exclusively on the *in*animate world.

The subjects depicted in *Twats, Cunts and Arseholes of England and Wales* are, as we can see, very much alive – if not to the mordant precept of their documentation. In fact, in some of the photographs they are so alive as to be apparently threatening the photographer with physical violence. In these photographs the subjects have quite possibly been provoked into action, and thus into unwitting compliance with Kilcline's titular premise. For the most part, though, we see genuine twats, cunts and arseholes going about their business. Most can be readily identified with a specific vocation. There are bank clerks, minicab drivers, fishmongers, hoteliers, butchers, janitors, electricians, librarians, lollipop men, acupuncturists, locksmiths, chefs, ware-house operatives, bus drivers, all demonstrating osten-sibly unsavoury behaviour almost certainly induced by the stress of their daily routine: a radiologist has been caught shouting at an elderly patient having difficulty climbing onto an MRI scanner; an enraged street-sweeper has been covertly snapped stamping his feet at the flyers, circulars, pizza leaflets and free local newspapers littered all around him; a balloon artist is seen fashioning guns, cutlasses and other inflatable weaponry for children in a cross-channel ferry's designated activity area. No fewer than four of the twats, cunts and arseholes can be identified as local-council civil servants/municipal factotums, while the remainder are either schoolchildren, students or vocationally indeterminate. Of this latter group, four are sprinting away from camera or shielding their faces behind one arm while making an obscene gesture with the other, while a fifth has both forearms over his face in a vertical position, like a boxer absorbing a flurry of punches. The other four vocationally indeterminate twats, cunts or arseholes are all armed with broken bottles, sticks and other appropriated offensive weapons (though interestingly these are not the ones apparently threatening the photographer with physical violence). One, bedecked in full Euro '96 England football kit, is shouting abuse at a policeman while restraining a Staffordshire bull terrier in a miniature St George's Cross cape from eating its own faeces. Another, a street drinker in his late thirties naked but for a pair of faded black Umbro football shorts and a Santa hat, is drunk at a school fête and being treated for minor head injuries by a team of St John Ambulance medics. The two others are identical twins wearing tabloid-issue T-shirts bearing the contorted features of former Nottingham Forest and England fullback Stuart Pearce in mid-goal celebration, his temples bulging in vascular catharsis.

Kilcline has resisted the temptation to include such maligned vocations as property consultants and traffic wardens – presumably because it has become passé to express disdain for them. Exactly how the nationality of the Welsh contingent is to be verified is anyone's guess; we will just have to take Kilcline's word for it. I thought I recognized a truculent ferry operative seen many times before at Fishguard Harbour, but this person could just as easily have been an Irishman from County Wexford, as the ferry – which sails to Rosslare and back twice daily – is crewed by both Welsh and Irish. In which case I would question the veracity of the piece's title.

At least three of the photographs are "infiltrated snap-shots"; that is to say, a passer-by has leapt impulsively into the frame making a thumbs-up gesture and sporting a sarcastically cheesy grin at the exact moment of the shutter's release. Due to the advent of the digital camera this practice is now in decline, twats[1] of this kind having long since been given to understand that the tourist will simply delete the infiltrated snapshot and aim the camera once more at the Cenotaph or the Gherkin or whichever monument/important building has captured his imagination. Kilcline has lamented the increasing scarcity of photographs whose subject is unplanned or unintentional or mediated by unforeseen circumstances. He has also inveighed against the digital camera's tendency to take the fun out of the whole photographic process, its tendency to encourage the editing of pictures at source and the immediate comparison of photo to subject – the upshot of which is that all pictures taken with our invariably cheap, low-resolution model (especially those taken by other members of our family) must be subjected to continual aesthetic approval if they are to be retained as megabyte-hungry files. The process thus becomes freighted with ersatz professionalism. We begin to think of the results less as our snapshots and more as "a body of work": we compose, we construct – *we make art*. And there is certainly none of this "I can't wait to get my pictures developed".

---

1. Yes, *twats*, not "cunts", or "arseholes". A twat is someone whose behaviour is annoying but not malicious; an arsehole is someone whose behaviour may be perceived as malicious without intending to be so, while a cunt is someone who does everything within his power to make life worse for those around him.

Of the five "exfiltrated" photographs – i.e., those of people attempting to *evade* photographic capture – one contains only a blurred shoe and hand, middle finger uncurled in a textbook fuck-you expression. The obscene gestures captured in other photographs range from the more classically British "up yours" to a loose "five-knuckle shuffle", to a one-fingered "suck on this" salvo shot from the hip (which in both instances is accompanied by a Bugs Bunny-style overbite).

As to the people apparently threatening the photographer with physical violence, only by studying these photographs at length and comparing one with another does one gather that their wrath is directed not at the camera but at an unseen target behind it. Contextual similarities between certain individual photographs leads the (discerning) viewer to the unmistakable conclusion that this target can, in fact, only be one of the protagonists featured in another of the photographs showing people running at the camera threatening physical violence: these protagonists have been provoked into action not by Kilcline but by *one another*. It becomes apparent that Kilcline has simply placed himself in the centre of an existing dispute and snapped both combatants as they advance towards one another at a dead run with escalating fury and self-righteousness. Of these seven combatants, three look like the kind who, quite frankly, you would expect to know better, the kind you'd expect to be able to placate the most volatile of antagonists with calm, reasoned appeal to common sense; the kind who would, for example, give way on major trunk roads to obviously speeding traffic joining the slow lane from a hazardous slip road *without* immediately giving chase with savage intent (*à la* convicted road-rage murderer Kenneth Noye). Two, in suits, look testy but not tasty (the ensuing altercation probably unfolding as nothing more than the kind of shoving match often described by football pundits as "handbags"), while another, a thick-wristed water-cooler delivery guy with stubby dreads, looks like he enjoys an at least ninety-per-cent success rate in instances of routine male violence, without allowing the other ten percent of unsuccessful bouts to dent his machismo. But didn't I say there were seven combatants… which leaves one either without an opponent or engaged in two-against-one combat. Well, the seventh combatant advancing seemingly towards the camera at a dead run is quite clearly, obviously, unmistakably, beyond the shadow of a doubt, a seasoned professional hard man or some kind of ex-prizefighter, the target of whose fury is actually the earlier-mentioned person with his arms raised as if to evade photographic documentation (making him appear initially more like a "fifth exfiltrator" than an "eighth combatant") but in reality to protect himself from actual physical battery. Look carefully and we can see the prizefighter's shadow creeping into the bottom left-hand corner of the frame.

I can't believe I forgot to say that the poster features no women. Am I out on a limb or are the words "twat", "cunt" and "arsehole" strangely non-unisex? Has anyone yet set down on paper the curious inapplicability of "twat", "cunt" and "arsehole" to womankind?[2] Who among us has not, at some point, aimed one of these insults at someone and then mentally retracted it on discovering the malefactor's gender to be female? Such volte-face are most certainly not expressions of patronizing chivalry: it's not that the woman in question is undeserving of the vituperative intensity we may associate with "twat", "cunt" or "arsehole", but that these expletives, used so frequently in male-on-male altercations, seem semantically inappropriate for the expression of transgender invective – as though the lexicon of profanity lacks a whole panoply of feminine equivalents. Or maybe it is just not possible for men to hate women as much as they hate one another, which is to say, themselves... On the subject of which, *there*, sure enough, *is Kilcline himself*, in the bottom right-hand corner of the poster smoking a cigarette, doing nothing particularly reproachable but doubtless thinking all manner of mean-spirited things. Perhaps this inclusion of himself in the work is his first faltering step towards rehabilitation, for the gesture says more than most misanthropists are willing to admit: that a

2. *Postscript*: Not until three years after writing this article did I see that famous episode of *Curb Your Enthusiasm* in which Larry agrees to write the obituary for his wife's deceased aunt. An unfortunate typo results in the aunt being described not as "our beloved aunt" but as "our beloved cunt". There is the double – no, triple – shock of hearing not just a woman described as a cunt, not just an aunt described as a cunt, but a *dead* aunt described as a cunt. The scene's transgressive premium lies only partly in the obscenity of the word "cunt" and more primarily in its strange inappropriateness – which is exaggerated tenfold by the adjective "beloved".

loathing which encompasses such a broad cross section of humanity must spring from a loathing of one's own self.

But what's this? Doesn't that gentleman there in the adjacent photograph – the children's entertainer – bear more than a passing resemblance to the artist? And the radiologist – is there not something staged about his gesture of pained exasperation? Isn't that lollipop man something of a makeweight? Could it possibly be that the assembled twats, cunts and arseholes are in fact, if not one and the same person, then a band of "volunteers" whose insincere collusion is the sole redemption of an otherwise morally reprehensible undertaking?

– That England, 2002

The George Carnegie Award

You cannot have failed to notice the recent relaunching of the George Carnegie Award. I, for one, welcome its return; quite why the Carnegie was shelved in the first place is beyond me. Older readers may recall that I myself was shortlisted in '61, so the Carnegie has always been very dear to my heart.

Anyway, the award ceremony took place last Thursday evening at the John Bryson Memorial Hall in Newark. I spent the whole of that week beseeching Mr Whitstable to send someone up to Nottinghamshire. "Think about it," said I, "if *Interregnum* can find space for articles on subjects as diverse as coin-snatching, bagpipe sealant, Ostrobothnian chamber music and the euphonic virtues of the word 'apricot', it really ought to be able to find space for the 252nd George Carnegie Award for Best Use of a Semicolon in the English Language." The old dog finally relented: "I see your point, Sean. It shall be your privilege to cover the event."

So here – if you will allow me the journalist's rather annoying habit of slipping into the present tense to describe something that has already happened – I am.

And it *is* a privilege. The nominees for the 1996 George Carnegie Award are as follows:

1. Ruth Hamilton, from page 145 of her best-selling novel *Spinning Jenny*, which finds Henry Skipton, the "embittered, solitary man who took care never to see his invalid wife", observing Maria and Jenny from afar:

> Excitement seemed to bubble in the air above the two girls' heads; they were obviously discussing something of great interest and import.

The semicolon is here used as an indication of the physical and psychological distance between observer and observed. While, in this respect, Hamilton's entry *is* a fairly solid deployment, it feels far too perfunctory to command our full interest. The aimed-for intrigue and curiosity as to what, exactly, is being "discussed" is ham-fistedly telegraphed by the reflective pause that the semicolon is intended to convey. No, I'm sorry, a clear makeweight. Another time, Hamilton, another time.

2. Della Thompson, for this "multiple" from the Preface to the 1995 edition of the *Concise Oxford Dictionary*, in which the editor – perhaps unconsciously lamenting the Sisyphean nature of the lexicographer's task – informs us that this new edition contains a staggering

> …7,000 new words and senses in a wide variety of areas. For example, the growing availability of

international cuisine in Britain and elsewhere is reflected in the use in English of terms such as *bhaji*, *fajita*, *gravlax*, *penne*, *sharon fruit* and many others; in the field of politics we have *dream ticket*, *Euro-rebel*, *placeman*, *rainbow coalition* and *spin doctor*; in ecology new terms such as *arcology*, *carr*, *ecocide*, *greening* and *wind farm* have arisen; in science and medicine, *blue box*, *bronchodilator*, *Creutzfeldt-Jakob disease*, *Feynman diagram*, *hyperspace*, *NiCad*, *packet switching*, *repetitive strain injury* and *wormhole*.

Some people questioned the shortlisting of a reference author, so this entry had the pundits leafing through the history books for a precedent (none was found). Personally, I find its demure workmanship very enticing. Let me be the first to hail Thompson's nomination as a triumph for the many unsung custodians of the English language working in the reference field.

3. Randolph Stow: the dark horse in many critics' eyes. On page 25 of this Australian-born author's readable whodunnit, *The Suburbs of Hell*, the central character, Harry, expresses his fear that the villagers' paranoia can only be intensified by the most recent murder:

When he was alive he dint do nobody no harm; and now he's dead, he's goona tear this place apart.

Some members of the audience ventured the opinion that the semicolon somehow reveals Stow for the generic man o' letters he in fact is, that the unabashed "literariness" of the caesura sits uncomfortably with the vernacular transcription of the Norfolk dialect. Champions of the Patrick White Award-winning novelist countered that the semicolon is an *ideal* transcription of the verbal segues encountered within English's more obscure dialects. Aside from this, you would've thought that both camps must surely have been united in their admiration for the part the semicolon here plays in inaugurating the ensuing psychological warfare: "in life a harmless yokel; in death a divider of villagers' loyalties, a pointer of fingers at shifty vergers and apparently motiveless Good Companions Club treasurers." But no, they were not united. "The victim's corpse," insisted a rather catty minority, "is here brought metaphorically back to life for the secondary resuscitation of an ailing plot" – which I thought was meandering rather disingenuously from the point. This debate over the punctuational gentrification of vernacular dialogue is surely one that will run and run.

4. Angela Kilmartin, for this effort from her acclaimed self-help manual, *Understanding Cystitis*:

> Urologists seldom examine the vagina – it's not their realm; neither do gynaecologists care much about the urethra.

Hmm. I don't know about you, but I always find a dashed clause of this kind more convincing when consolidated with a full stop; when followed by a semicolon, its efficacy can seem somewhat diminished due to the reader being ushered on to the next part of the sentence. While technically on the money, the dash and the semicolon conspire to create an ungainly parenthesis which, like a man rubbing his tummy and patting his head at the same time, is having difficulty trying to accomplish two things at once. Surely the tart recrimination of "– it's not their realm" merits the detachment of a full parenthesis? The sentence dares us to rewrite it, perhaps with the dashed clause at the end:

> Urologists seldom examine the vagina; neither do gynaecologists care much about the urethra – it's not their realm.

Since Kilmartin suggests that both the gynaecologist and the urologist are *equally* wary of straying from their respective realms, the displacement of "– it's not their realm" from the middle to the end of the sentence does not compromise the information it is intended to convey. And the semicolon, more importantly, is now free to exhibit its defining characteristic; that is, a subtlety of deviation and turn of pace the like of which other punctuation marks *can only dream*. (A word of advice, Kilmartin: if you're going to go to the trouble of opening up a parenthesis, then for Heaven's sake let the reader bask in it. Like a company director taking half an hour out of a hectic business schedule to read a paperback in a global coffee franchise, a good parenthesis should stand aloof from, while retaining an awareness of, the hustle and bustle of the larger sentence of which it is a part.)

Am I being harsh? Maybe. I will say only that, when it comes to the Carnegie, better authors than Kilmartin have been found wanting.

5. Ron Atkinson, for this charming *faux naïf* bricolage from his memoir *Big Ron: A Different Ball Game*:

> ...Finally there is Paul McGrath, but I don't know what you would call him – English because he was born in London; Irish because he played for them; or black because that's what he is!

What can I say? Fans of the beautiful game may recall that as manager of West Bromwich Albion in the mid to late '70s, Atkinson was responsible for nurturing the first high-profile generation of black players to grace football's top echelon. Cyrille Regis, Brendan Batson and Lawrie Cunningham (whom Atkinson collectively nicknames The Three Degrees) are given an entire chapter in this book – in which, generally, I have to say, semicolons are tossed around with the abandon of a pub team hoisting hopeful but easily dealt-with centres into the box. The author is at his most candid in this chapter; his anxious attempts to square football's institutionally racist past with his own (stated) contempt for political correctness make especially fascinating reading. I commend his publisher for maintaining such faith in the project.

The refreshingly frank – and apparently unghosted – prose of *Big Ron: A Different Ball Game* is of an altogether more experimental nature than that of the other nominees, and the semicolon almost has the feel of a trained infantry parachuted in to facilitate the author's decidedly guerrilla manœuvres: note how he confronts the difficulty of assessing McGrath's racial identity by damming up its indeterminacy behind semicolons until he can hold back the truth no longer. When the truth finally dawns on the author, it does so with a sense of factual hysteria: "...black because that's what he is!" Outstanding.

6. Hampton Fancher and David Peoples, for this famous piece of dialogue from their screenplay to Ridley Scott's *Blade Runner*:

It's too bad she won't live; but then again, who does?

I know, it's a shame isn't it? Despite the obvious short-comings of their work I felt sorry for the other nom-inees – I mean, none of them stood a chance. In perhaps the bitterest controversy to dog the Carnegie since James Joyce's astonishing posthumous nomination of 1946, first prize was awarded to Fancher and Peoples. It turned out that, after much "behind-the-scenes acrimony" and "last-ditch crisis talks" between the sponsors of the award and its steering committee, screenplays had finally been given the nod a mere two days before the nominations were supposed to be in. Had Ridley Scott – late-night media anchormen asked the nation – the esteemed director of, amongst other box office triumphs, *Alien* and *Thelma & Louise*, *really* been cynically lobbied to persuade his collaborators on *Blade Runner* to step in to enhance the Carnegie's low profile? And had, as some of the more libellous cultural commentators weighed in to suggest, the semicolon *really* been inserted only in a last-minute revision of the original text? The *Guardian* not only insisted that this was indeed the case (its editorial in typically studied disagreement with the wider broadsheet consensus, which stuck to the bland assertion that the competition had merely entered a new era, widening its remit to reflect an "expanded concept of literary excellence in our cross-media cultural landscape") but brought the public's attention to the (in its eyes) still more heinous crime of the selectors having "the audacity to skirt the issue of the legitimacy of Fancher and Peoples' nomination by claiming to have based their decision on the more recent 1992 director's cut… [which], though it *does* fall within the mandatory ten-year window of production stipulated in the guide for nominations, could hardly be said to offer a sufficiently different version to the original to merit a prize of the Carnegie's so-called integrity."

In my opinion it is difficult to imagine a weaker shortlist with which to have relaunched the Carnegie (just for the record, '61 saw me drawn against Waugh,

Greene and Eliot), so it should surprise no one that a work of *Blade Runner*'s profile should clinch the award. It *was* a bit disappointing that the winners could not be persuaded to receive the award in person or even express their gratitude via satellite link-up. Such, I suppose, is the humility of the screenplay writer. In their absence it fell to Ridley Scott himself to address the audience from an undisclosed location in Central America, where he is currently shooting his new film. This he did very graciously: swinging from a hammock and nursing an ice-cold Michelob, the venerated auteur held laconically forth for several seconds on the pleasures of receiving further recognition for a work that had initially been unfavourably compared to the more accessible (and certainly less Fritz Lang-influenced) *E.T.*, before the screen flickered and malfunctioned, the director's suave platitudes lost in a crepitation of static.

– *Interregnum*, 1996

Brick Lane Market

Tourists, why put money in the pockets of smarmy West End shysters offering TAX-FREE DISCOUNTS TO HOLDERS OF A NON-BRITISH PASSPORT when you can get a *real* piece of London down at Brick Lane Market? Every Sunday, control of the lane is ceded to the various cockneys and mockneys still trying to eke out a living in the East End. My advice is to arrive early, as most of the bargains have been snapped up by one o'clock. Bric-a-brac stalls abound, as do vintage-clothes emporia and incense booths. Dank, crepuscular lock-ups disgorge rotting furniture, rusty hand tools and ancient stereophonic vinyl onto the street. Characters too numerous to mention would have Dickens ransacking his brain for adjectives: the stumpy Venezuelan in his endearing van crammed with aphoristic mouse mats, the remaindered-calculator salesman on Sclater Street; everywhere, men three generations apart haggling over pornography. Should the visitor tire of the more traditional stalls (the fruiterer's shrill vernacular can be especially trying), then contraband tobacconists, itinerant SIM-card sharps and numerous other black marketeers all lie in wait to accompany those tourists looking to get off the beaten track to the nearest ATM.

This, then, is the general flavour. I have to say, though, that the further one strays from the centre of the mar- ket – which is to be found where Cheshire Street crosses Brick Lane – the more interesting it becomes. The most fascinating part is the stretch by the junction of Bethnal Green Road and Commercial Street. Here it is possible to find stalls comprising nothing more than a Genesis cassette and the limbs of a broken doll balanced carefully on a window ledge. Continue up Commercial Street and you will eventually encounter a collection of objects – say, a beer mat, bike spanner and a filthy romper suit – that may or may not be a "stall". Next to which there will be another collection of objects – a mulch of mildewed popsocks and piss-soaked saris – that one hopes isn't. The end of the market? Not a chance; like a dynamite fuse that won't be stamped out, it continues, unwanted detritus blending artfully back into merchandise. Any object, no matter how abject, is imbued with a last-ditch existential insistence, steadfastly resisting demotion to the rank of mere mat- ter: biro cap, colander, Curtis Stigers calendar – the only virtue these objects have is that they still exist. That a warped "black plastic disc" may happen to have a spiral groove running from the circumference to its centre, encrypting a selection of ballads by Phil Collins, is but a footnote to its nominal signification of "space that is not yet empty".

A friend of mine once offered to buy a proprietor's entire stall for a considerably generous sum (with the intention of exhibiting it as a readymade artwork). Of course, he refused – confirming my friend's suspicions that the proprietor considered it his purpose, his vocation, his métier, not to *sell* the objects he had before him but *to keep them in the world for as long as possible*. To sell, you see, would profane the catechistic ritual of self-affirmation that his stall facilitates, a ritual that might be summarized thus: "Despite the obsolescence of the things I have before me, *my own obsolescence has not yet come*." His merchandise resonates with the deferral of his own oblivion.

Anyway, the residual effect on the beholder of this shuddering proprietary nominalism is such that, as he walks the next twenty yards back up Commercial Street (passing one seemingly final outpost after another with much the same trepidation as Poe's Arthur Gordon Pym passed "the parallel of Bennet's Islet... a region of novelty and wonder..."), his eyes seem to transfigure crisp packets, beer cans, bricks, broken bottles and sticks into promising commercial viabilities. This is natural, for he has been mesmerized by the entrepreneurial witchcraft of London's desperately poor and doesn't want the market to end, wants it to continue in the same entropic fashion, just to see how bad it can get, how little it can dwindle to while still retaining a mercantile imperative. He longs for the further commodification of dust and rubble, desiccated dogshit and vomit; for the renovation of filthy nooks and crannies into enticing sideshows where street drinkers are paid to scream abuse into the ears of smiling Japanese tourists.

Let us admit that the visitor to Brick Lane Market (which can be reached by taking the District Line to Aldgate East) yearns to see capitalism carried to its logical conclusion: the curdled old tramp peddling spit in a bag for tuppence; the mysterious broken man, who has nothing more to sell than an onion and the story of how he came to butcher his lurcher for the amusement of some passing *faux*hemians.

– *The Sardinian*, 1999

Public Brothels 1975–85

Since 1962 the National Brothel Association has issued
several books detailing new brothels in the United
Kingdom. The previous volume, published in 1976,
was edited by Rupert Chase and covered the relatively
short period 1971–74. In retrospect, the production of
this volume was somewhat hurried and ill conceived,
Chase himself admitting that, due to a combination of
financial constraints and a tight publishing schedule,
several of the 169 regional brothel authorities had not
been consulted on recent developments in their area.
In most people's eyes, however, Chase atoned for these
oversights the following year at the conference *Brothel Design: Recent Trends*, giving a diligent appraisal
of projects omitted from his 1976 volume and also
offering some editorial advice on the production of
future volumes. This conference, organized with the
assistance of the Shepway and Thanet Branch of the
National Brothel Association (of which Chase is the
chairman), helped to revive interest in a neglected area
of municipal-architecture-reference-book publishing.
While there has always been a modest readership for our
ongoing series of publications, Chase's paper seemed to
mark a turning point, for in recent years public curiosity

and affection for previous volumes has snowballed into demand for a new one. Many are indebted to Mr Chase's reinvigoration of the field; we are doubly so, for it is to his affiliation with Shepway and Thanet that we owe the generous financial assistance given to produce this volume. Without this assistance it is likely that we would have seen the end of the series.

Rupert Chase also found us an editor-in-chief. This was none other than Howard Goodman, who, as keynote speaker at Chase's conference of seven years earlier and a revered figure in the world of municipal-architecture-reference-book publishing, had already proposed a volume initially designed to cover the years 1975–82. Mr Goodman had never actively sought financial sponsorship for this project – which had by his own admission become more of a hobby than a vocational imperative, due to escalating work commitments – and it took a chance meeting with Chase at the 1984 East Anglia Agricultural Show to rekindle his interest in it. His work as fund-raiser and matchmaker done, Rupert Chase then retreated with typical modesty into the background, leaving Howard Goodman and myself to devise a work-able publishing schedule. Sadly, no sooner had we done so than Mr Goodman's work commitments escalated still further, and his involvement in the project became unfeasible. Adam Redgrave, an academic colleague and friend of Howard Goodman, and an authority on municipal architecture in his own right, then agreed to step in and edit the volume, which had now to cover the period 1975–85. Howard Goodman immediately handed over to him information he had been collecting since 1975, a gesture praised and lamented in equal measure: praised for the obvious generosity of allowing others to profit by one's own research, and lamented because it seemed to mark a clean break between Howard G. Goodman and the world of municipal-architecture-reference-book publishing.

If my brief association with Howard Goodman afforded an insight into probably the greatest mind in municipal-architecture-reference-book-publishing history, then my longer association with Adam Redgrave afforded an insight into surely the next-greatest. Redgrave quickly perceived that the collection of the data necessary for the kind of book originally envisaged by Goodman and myself was too big a task for two men, so he enlisted the help of three associate editors, C.H. Anscombe, J.L. Cartwright and I.T. Coolidge. He also called, at my suggestion, on the services of Miss V.S. Bishop, architecture and sex-industry consultant to the editors of the 1968 and 1976 volumes. This group first met in December 1985, when it was agreed to divide up the 169 UK brothel authorities between the four panellists. All UK brothel authorities were requested to supply details of new premises opened between 1st January 1975 and 31st December 1985. While awaiting this information, the panel made pilot assessments of Basingstoke Central Brothel and Sleaford and Rochester brothels to establish more precisely the criteria to be surveyed and thereby ensure maximum commensurability among the chosen examples.

It took much longer than we had envisaged to decide which examples to feature, for in order to agree on the criteria to be examined, the editorial panel was obliged to widen the remit of its pilot visits to include several brothel authorities that had not answered its correspondence, or that had done so in somewhat cursory manner. Of the 169 designated public-brothel authorities written to, no replies were received from eighteen, while twenty responded, reporting that no new brothels had been opened since 1975. The panel, who had information to the contrary (Howard Goodman's preliminary research proving invaluable here), were thus obliged to carry out fieldwork in many of these thirty-eight "fugitive" authorities. It is as well they did, for the results gathered enhance the current volume beyond measure, as is evidenced by the entries on Bedford, Kettering and Tring.

The other 131 authorities were more forthcoming (some even offering to liaise with their uncooperative counterparts), and the panel eventually collated a staggering 784 projects. Some of these were extensions and conversions, but the majority were new, purpose-built brothels. Clearly, visiting all these projects would have further delayed the already overdue publication, so – notwithstanding Mr Redgrave's repeated offer to undertake the bulk of visits himself – it was decided to write to the managers of major public brothels asking them to earmark the most outstanding establishments in their area. Not only did this prove an effective method of pre-selection, but the detailed information gleaned from the resulting correspondence led to a pivotal moment in the volume's evolution, for it became apparent that, while the best brothels were in most cases those that met every element of the panel's generic criteria, an establishment might also be worthy of inclusion by virtue of certain unique characteristics. For instance, if it scored badly with regard to lighting, ventilation or a badly asphalted disabled ramp, it could redeem itself with a well-designed reception desk (Harrogate), bespoke bathroom fixtures (Cannock Divisional), or with the uniform of its security staff (Louth). It was agreed to incorporate these "autochthonous" characteristics into the existing criteria, inserting a "Special Features" category to send out the clear message that, as far as the editorial panel of the 1985 volume of *Public Brothels* was concerned, particularity and even eccentricity were by no means anathema to the standardization and consistency that has characterized previous volumes in the series. "Indeed," wrote Mr Coolidge in his status report to Shepway and Thanet, "they may even complement it." When all this correspondence had been completed, the editorial panel drew up a preliminary shortlist of brothels to be visited.

A year later, no sooner had this programme of visits concluded than disaster – double disaster – struck. In late December 1986 Adam Redgrave suffered a severe stroke while returning from one of the local authorities in his remit. He passed away in hospital in the New Year. Having swiftly pledged to dedicate the volume to Mr Redgrave, the editorial panel appealed to a now retired

Howard Goodman to oversee the final editorial duties
– little suspecting that Goodman's own health was in
rapid decline; little suspecting, indeed, that the world
of municipal-architecture-reference-book publishing
was to lose two key figures in as many months.

One of Goodman's last contributions to the world of
municipal-architecture-reference-book publishing was
to telephone each member of the editorial panel to tell
them that they could do far worse than install the present
writer as editor-in-chief. Flattered and daunted in equal
measure, at the end of July 1987 I was able to collect
Adam Redgrave's papers and verify that all shortlisted
brothels in his catchment area – as well as a few others
in some of the more uncooperative regional authorities
– had been visited. Fortunately, Mr Redgrave had typed
out his meticulous assessments of brothels soon after
visiting them, awarding scores out of five in each of the
relevant categories, and this information was sufficient
to determine which ones merited full description and
which ones would be merely listed in the appendix
at the end of the volume. Without Adam Redgrave's
foresight, the book would have been further delayed,
and perhaps even compromised in its architectural
purview and the consistency of its attention to detail.
Furthermore, Mr Redgrave had taken it upon himself
to take photographs of façades, interiors, furnishings
and employees engaged in the duties characteristic of
the day-to-day running of a modern public brothel,
some of which, argued Miss Bishop, merited inclusion

in the volume alongside those commissioned from John Meadowcroft of Lombard Associates.

The panel agreed that Redgrave's portfolio would indeed add richness to the volume – and corroborate some of the more unusual claims made in the "Special Features" categories. The theme of "diversity" was one that preoccupied and even troubled us; our original intention to include brothels of *all* types, public or private, had been frustrated by our failure to secure the services of an actual brothel area manager, someone who travelled around a lot and had a thorough knowledge of just what exactly was out there. At a meeting in August 1987 the panel finally had to face the fact that, even if such a consultant could be appointed at this late stage, the time required for them to prosecute a full survey would only delay publication further and test to its absolute limit the patience and generosity of our benefactors at Shepway and Thanet. It was this, and no little fear that our vacillations might lead to our book being trumped by a rival volume, that led us to the regrettable decision to exclude all non-public brothels. Although this rendered immediately superfluous half of the work undertaken by our late editor-in-chief, the panel believes that this was the only way of reducing the survey to a manageable number. Regrettably, we have also had to exclude brothels aimed at a specific social demographic. Nevertheless, we like to imagine that there is, somewhere, an editorial panel working on a "sister volume" to our own: one dedicated to all those brothels – corporate, military, special-needs, not to mention those recently introduced by the government to cater solely for the homeless, asylum-seekers and people in receipt of state benefits – that lie beyond the remit of our own volume. Such a work would be a welcome addition to the canon.

Having given a background to this volume's evolution, let us now consider some recent trends in brothel design over the last decade. Two things have affected public-brothel building in this country more than any other: the 1974 reorganization of English and Welsh local government and advances in technology. These two factors conspired to usher in a difficult period, not just for brothel design and construction, but for the design and construction of any municipal building. A significant number of the brothels included in this volume had lain on the drawing board since 1973, when the impending rationalization of local government seemed to impel many ailing authorities to spend up all their capital at once: for the benefit, so they claimed, of their ratepayers, but in reality, one suspects, to create a lasting legacy of their tenure. It is true that more brothels were commissioned under the latter half of Edward Heath's administration than in any other period; it is also true that few were immediately built, the main reason being the political hiatus between the hung parliament of the 1974 February general election and the formation of Harold Wilson's government in October of that same year – a hiatus that should have provided a period of reflection, a time for political neutrals to step in and review plans that had been drawn up by one administration only to be meddled with by its successor.

Instead, it seems to have ushered in a period of pro-crastination and managerial imprudence. The biggest oversight was the complete failure to anticipate the introduction of computer technology and make the required adjustments to the electrical circuits of the original designs, and to anticipate the knock-on spatial and ergonomic problems caused by the proliferation of power supplies. Each of the local brothel authorities, it seems, was waiting for the others to take the lead. It is easy, in our age of word processors, fax machines and touch-tone telephones, to berate such procrastination, but we should try to see things from the perspective of a brothel manager in 1975: had there *been* any informa-tion-technology consultants, occupational therapists and disability-access advisors to commission reports from, then the necessary changes could have been made with a minimum of fuss. Had these vocational fields not been in their infancy, then who knows how many of the current inadequacies could have been avoided? The woeful shortage of supply points to accommodate the exponential proliferation of electrically powered equipment was just one of many gripes of the early 1980s brothel manager, and this period saw the in-trays of local authorities awash with applications for renovation grants. The cost of which, we need hardly add, was ultimately borne by the same ratepayers who had funded the overzealous brothel commissioning of the Heath years.

Of all the eras of civic reconstruction, the post-Second World War rebuilding programme has attracted the most criticism. Immediately after the war, when the priority was merely to house as many people as quickly and as efficiently as possible, development of any kind was welcomed; it was only from the mid-'50s onwards – when the byword was "*re*development" and "radicalism became the norm" (to quote Howard Goodman) – that planners began to run riot. Immense tracts of inner-city housing stock and old high-street commercial premises were razed to the ground, many brothels being forced to relocate to unfamiliar districts, where they faced an uncertain future. This relocation programme was at best perfunctory and at worst punitive, many of the decamped brothels falling quickly into disuse and eventual closure due to local indifference or competition from existing establishments. The few inner-city brothels left standing were hit by a second wave of redevelopment in the mid-'60s, when many old and noteworthy examples were demolished instead of being listed for their architectural beauty. While these establishments still thrived due to a new influx of commuter clients, there was little or no local patronage to galvanize resistance to the then Minister for Housing and Local Government Richard Crossman's policy of compulsory purchase. The few who did speak out against Crossman's persecution of these "unsightly anachronisms" could do little to counter the argument that the renovation of these old buildings would be far trickier and less cost-efficient than building completely new ones. But fashions can change quickly, and by the late '60s it was acknowledged that mistakes had been made, that developers had indeed been given too long a leash. By the mid-'70s the trend had been halted, if not quite reversed. While the majority of the 784 brothels opened between 1975 and 1985 were completely new buildings, a small but significant proportion were successful – and in some cases award-winning – conversions of once maligned "anachronisms".

Of all the other trends that the panel has commented on, the increasing number of dual-use brothels is perhaps the most intriguing. As early as 1978 Howard Goodman observed that "the provision of state-subsidized sexual gratification alongside such other civic amenities as Citizens' Advice Bureaux, tourist-information centres, labour exchanges and even libraries is now commonplace". Nottinghamshire, Berkshire and Gwent were initially the leading authorities in this respect, though as Rupert Chase pointed out in his introduction to the previous volume, it is a trend that British brothels seem to have imported from Scandinavia, where the requisite legislation was in place a full forty years before its UK equivalent.

In some quarters dual-use has received a mixed reception, most notably from the managers of academic brothels, who report a reluctance among fee-paying students to share campus facilities with the wider community. But this resistance of further- and higher-education brothels to dual-use is in stark contrast to the initiatives of many comprehensive schools, which have demonstrated that a brothel provided for use by both community and school can be efficient, cost-effective and even profitable. Such initiatives are not restricted to urban areas; the school brothel has even thrived in small village communities, where there is insufficient council revenue to devote a separate building to each amenity. There are even hamlets in places such as Northumberland and Dumfries and Galloway that, though bereft of a school house from which to run a brothel, nevertheless strive to offer a service on certain days of the week, usually in a room in a public house, post office or general store. In fact, this is commonplace in island communities, as can be seen by our entry on the Western Isles detailing a whole network of "brothel surgeries", many of which operate out of local distilleries.

Such enterprise makes sense in remote, rural communities, but there is a growing band of sceptics who have misgivings about the free market ethos that the dual-use brothel seems to engender in urban contexts: dual-use, they argue, can too quickly become multi-use. The revenue generated by the hire of conference rooms, art galleries, cafés and bingo halls has to be carefully and honestly managed, so that state-sponsored institutions do not become exploited by renegade privateers. Commerce must remain a by-product of brothel-management, not become its *raison d'être*: "enterprising" managers should not be allowed to create a "money-changers in the temple" scenario. While, to our knowledge, no brothel area manager has yet overturned a bingo table or cash register in anger, many in the industry would welcome new government legislation clarifying exactly what would constitute unethical use of brothel premises.

On a more practical note, architects and brothel managers have complained about the inadequate designs of reception desks since this series began in 1952. Designers counter that existing difficulties have been compounded by computerization and the introduction of unwieldy automated debiting systems; that they had only just begun to address these difficulties when the introduction of this equipment exacerbated the problem. But the editors of this volume, having seen many examples of various kinds and listened to staff bemoan the ergonomic shortcomings of often ludicrously elaborate designs, cannot help but feel that now is the perfect time to review the whole process of reception-desk design. Our research indicates – overwhelmingly – that designers are addressing the problem from an overly aesthetic viewpoint, and we think that the introduction of the automated equipment may, far from "making an already difficult task impossible", provide the necessary constraint for the development of more user-friendly models. In fact, designers are already consulting with employees. We may, it seems, finally be turning the corner; we may even be halfway to establishing some industry standards regarding working heights and legroom, one of many recent trade-union demands. The reader will not be surprised to learn that this collaboration was first mooted in a plan for radical overhauls drawn up in 1982 by Adam Redgrave in consultation with Howard Goodman.

The editors agree that it will take more than an intervention from beyond the grave by the sorely missed doyens of municipal-architecture-reference-book publishing to solve another problem that is undermining the efficient management of brothels nationwide: the loss of equipment. The security systems which many brothels have been forced to install at reception exits to combat theft range from sophisticated devices that sound an alarm triggered by tagged equipment to simple trays in which patrons are required to deposit their bags for the duration of their visit. John Meadowcroft's documentation of a number of examples (figs. 32–41) shows that whatever solution is adopted, it usually has a detrimental effect on an otherwise thoughtfully designed interior, and it would seem that the invention of an unobtrusive system is some way off yet.

On a slightly more upbeat note, since the publication of the 1976 volume, many older brothels have increased their maintenance efficiency – mainly due to a 1977 directive stipulating new targets for maintenance contractors. As to the upkeep of brand-new buildings, a key criterion of the project managers who built them was the selection of materials and methods as much for ease and economy of maintenance as for cosmetic appearance. While this volume does its utmost to showcase those examples which, in its opinion, strike a balance between architectural flair and utilitarian pragmatism, we have also included some examples that illustrate how an obsession with function and efficiency can lead to a disregard for the "feel-good factor" necessary to guarantee the regular return of patrons. We have also deliberately included projects which advanced esoteric architectural claims that we believe have been all but discredited. Let us admit that the desire to assert form over function has sometimes resulted in the perpetuation of false economies. For example, in the early 1980s architects tended to spurn air conditioning as an unsightly encumbrance to the "formal harmony" of their designs, but this formal harmony has invariably been compromised by the very palliative measures introduced in its absence – often, we should point out, at a greater cumulative cost than the original plans for air conditioning. We can only hope that brothel authorities will learn fast from these mistakes and try to strike a balance between idealism and pragmatism, between thriftiness and false economy: for in too many cases inadequate construction budgets have – be it in the hands of misguided idealists or cautious realists – resulted in problems that will only be rectified by wholesale renovation.

The reader should not make the mistake of assuming that the fully described brothels are necessarily superior to those that have merely been listed; in fact, for every brothel fully described, there is probably another in the same region worthy of inclusion in the final shortlist. The editorial panel had originally hoped to include somewhere in the region of 300 brothels, but when financial constraints made it apparent that only 200 could be given comprehensive descriptive treatment, we had to find a way of reducing the figure. The first criterion obviously had to be geographical: a reference volume of this nature has a responsibility to include examples from all regions of the UK. We acknowledge that certain individual brothel authorities could have contributed a great many more projects to the main part of the volume, but at least all 784 have been listed in the appendix. To return to the issue of diversity, the final selection represents brothels of many shapes and sizes, from the huge park-and-ride development in West Bromwich to Guildford's recent Community Brothel extension, to the Wayfarers' Brothel in Saham Toney, Norfolk – and not forgetting, of course, those tiny "brothel surgeries" mentioned earlier. Incidentally, the smallest self-contained brothel listed is a converted public convenience in New Basford, Nottingham, measuring a mere 20' x 22'. I fear that record may not last long, for I recently received a leaflet from a representative of Staffordshire County Council announcing plans for a fleet of mobile brothels as part of a community outreach initiative. We wish them the best of luck with their project – and look forward to featuring these peregrinatory trailblazers in future volumes.

On behalf of the editorial panel, I should like to thank all the brothel managers and their staff for their unstinting cooperation, personal warmth and willingness to supply us with the correct information. We know that, in some cases, this entailed a search for documents that did not in fact exist, and we appreciate the diligence with which so many of you undertook to unearth useful material, compile fresh statistics and even photograph details that we had overlooked in our zeal to complete the project. Our gratitude is due also to the many architects and original project managers – many of whom have now retired – who answered our correspondence and agreed to participate in our evaluative surveys.

My special thanks go to the associate editors, C.H. Anscombe, J.L. Cartwright and I.T. Coolidge, and to Miss V.S. Bishop, Henry Woolnough, S.W. Saunders and Norman Atwood for their continual support. Contributions by Adrian Gedge, A.D. Callaghan, Kevin Wing, O.C. Claxton, Steve Bonding and I.S.W.T. Pilkington are also gratefully acknowledged, as is the patience and forbearance of our good friends at the Shepway and Thanet Branch of the National Brothel Association, Rupert Chase RIBA, Jo Akehurst, Phillip Wright, Peter Davis and Christopher John Sutton-Westall, who have offered not only their financial backing but far more practical guidance than we could reasonably have expected. Thanks also to Michael Davenport, Rosemary Pointer, Keith Denton, Jon Whittaker, Don Irwin, Miss P.L. Coote, Bryan Buchanan, Neil Osborne, Roger Garment, Dr Blaine Repton and Stuart Ostler, who all attended the editorial panel's meetings on behalf of Shepway and Thanet, and to Marcus Armitage, Dave Roote, Martin Baign,

Malcom G. Shawcross, P.J. Deville, Jane Reason, Ian Watt, D.J. Upritchard, R.S. Pitt, Nigel Stannard, John Measures, Dorothy Swalecliffe and Eileen Yarrow, all of whom fielded numerous telephone enquiries while the editorial panel was away conducting its research in the field; and finally to Richard Parfitt and Eric Sprawson at Dashford Typesetters, Jim Hubbard at Blasket Press in Bury St Edmunds, and John and Valerie Meadowcroft at Lombard Associates.

To say that the contributions of Adam Redgrave and Howard G. Goodman deserve something more than mere gratitude is an understatement. We hope the present volume is a fitting epitaph to their memory.

– Introduction to *Public Brothels 1975–85*, 1987

Trophy 2000–

I see that *Trophy* has resurfaced – after an absence of nearly a decade. Stolen in 2006 from a group show at Arnolfini, it was recently unearthed in an Ipswich branch of Cancer Research by the curator Gavin Wade. How it got there is unclear, though we can form a sketchy picture of its recent adventures from the list of recipients engraved on its base by its kidnappers. Yes, *kidnappers* – for followers of contemporary art will recall that a ransom was demanded at the time, a ransom far beyond the means of both gallery and artist.

I should explain that *Trophy* (or *Trophy 2000–*, to give it its full title) is a work made in 2000 by the artist Elizabeth Price. Here, for those of you who haven't a clue what I'm talking about, is a description of the piece I wrote fourteen years ago for *The Sardinian*:

> Elizabeth Price's *Trophy 2000–* is a stainless-steel trophy that, when displayed in a gallery or public space, is engraved with the venue's name and the exact date of its exhibition. In this way it recycles its exhibitory history as the material for the work, reducing itself to the simple provenance of its journey from one place to another. But this object – a symbol of

achievement and success – is hardly to be understood in terms of its being "awarded" to the gallerist/curator in recognition of a perceived cultural cachet; rather, it *condescends* to appear, taking its place among the other exhibits with an equivocal aloofness, a demure cultural inertia. To date, *Trophy 2000–* has appeared at Anthony Wilkinson Gallery, London (4th May–4th June 2000); Lenbachhaus Museum, Munich (22nd June–8th September 2002); Mobile Home Gallery, London (3rd May–8th June 2003); Houldsworth Fine Art, London (17th July–8th August 2003); and most recently at 1,000,000 mph, London (11th October–2nd November 2003). Anyone familiar with these venues will attest, I think, to their wide-ranging objectives. Having appeared in hardcore-commercial, artist-run and museum contexts alike, *Trophy 2000–* seems like a more social version of Robert Morris's 1963 piece *Location* (a two-foot-square board containing four numerical gauges set according to its position on the wall), metering a socio-geographical rather than spatial odyssey – and somehow reifying the objectives of each exhibitory context in the process. The viewer refers the most recent outing to its previous ones, reflecting on the propinquity of the various venues. The objectives of these venues differ markedly, and promise to diversify still further as the dynamic of the art world organically adapts to meet the increasingly eclectic needs of audience, artist and curator. The dash in *Trophy 2000–*'s title makes enigmatic reference to the open-ended, temporal nature of the piece, whose circulation will be brought to a seemingly arbitrary end when there is no room left for any more names to be engraved on its base. What is not so arbitrary is the history it will come to speak of, the status quo that must necessarily change – certain venues having long since disappeared and others having risen to more influential positions. Interestingly, in an age in which overexposure is often said to diminish the aura of cultural artefacts, the more *Trophy* is exhibited, the more effective it becomes: the accretion of ubiquity is its *raison d'être*. Price is quite happy for *Trophy* to go wherever it is wanted, and we can perhaps foresee a time when some more prestigious venues are added to those listed above, thus emphasizing the relative anonymity of less established recipients: in the same way that the European Cup, usually shared between such titans as Madrid, Milan and Munich, has occasionally found itself in the trophy cabinet of Steaua Bucharest or Aston Villa, so *Trophy* must deign to appear at places like Luton Central Library Concourse. One only hopes that Price's work doesn't fall foul of its roaming instincts; that, wherever it travels, it will be well guarded.

Portentous, those last words. Most football fans will be able to tell you that the FA Cup was stolen from a shop window display in 1895, and that the Jules Rimet trophy was pinched weeks before the 1966 World Cup (though it was recovered, with typically English sentimentality, by a dog named Pickles). Unlike the FA,

Price never issued a replacement for her stolen work, though presumably she has a record of its previous recipients and could have engraved their names onto a replica without too much trouble. That she did not turns out to have been a masterstroke, for judging by the names added to its base, *Trophy* seems to have had a far more picaresque time in its abductors' hands than in the art world. Some commentators have even suggested that Price engineered the whole thing herself in order to enrich the work, an accusation the artist has firmly refuted, though she admitted that the idea of "Stockholm Syndrome" – the phenomenon whereby abductor and abductee enter into a collaboration – was one that intrigued her on a philosophical level.

The illicit titivation of existing artworks has an interesting and varied history. Examples range from Hitler moustaches, marker-penned compulsively by schoolboys onto portraits of pompous dignitaries, to more premeditated projects, carefully planned operations that, far from merely sabotaging the work, try to extend – or at least engage with – the idea behind it. The most effective of these often subject the artist's "timeless" or "transcendental" gesture to a more concrete appraisal. Antony Gormley's *Angel of the North* has never looked finer than when draped with a giant 29' x 17' replica of Alan Shearer's No. 9 shirt by fanatical Newcastle United fans in 1998, and some have suggested that only with this gesture was Gormley's commission accepted as the psychogeographical icon its title claims it to be. To suggest that, for the Toon Army, the *Angel*'s outstretched arms are now permanently transfigured into those of a striker in mid-goal celebration (admittedly, a celebration more reminiscent of former Tottenham Hotspurs and Germany striker Jürgen Klinsmann's "aeroplane dive" than Shearer's more prosaic one-fingered salute) is not to pander to a "proletariat redemption" of high culture; it is merely to suggest that the hierarchical distinction between high and low culture sometimes dissolves into a symbiosis, whereby what begins as the former finds a more lucid expression as the latter. Snobs usually disparage the outcome as bathos, but true art lovers know the work of a poet when they see it. And poetry is what they will see if they visit the Institute of Contemporary Art's new headquarters in Biggleswade, where *Trophy* will shortly go on display as the first in an ongoing acquisition of contemporary British works. Housed in a purpose-built alcove carved into the ICA's granite foyer, *Trophy* has now retired from public life. Where she has been, what she has seen – on these points I am sworn to secrecy. The confidentiality agreement critics were required to sign before viewing the work permits me to disclose no more than is stated in the current press release: that *Trophy* was initially taken to a derelict castle on Lundy; that she was once spotted on the counter of an engravers in Leipzig; that at some point in spring of 2016 she was secreted in the hold of a Dutch trawler bound for Lowestoft. If you want to fill in the blanks, why not take a drive up to Bedfordshire?

– *The Plastic Arts*, 2017

Fruit Hosiery

When *Playboy* was launched in 1953, it announced itself as "a gentlemen's club in print form". Alongside pictures of naked women were features that straddled the worlds of fashion, sport, music, cinema – even literature. Writers as revered as Vladimir Nabokov and Margaret Atwood have contributed to *Playboy*, and such is its proportion of erotic to cultural content that any youngster discovering a copy in his father's stash of mucky books is likely to baulk at the surprisingly low acreage of skin. Across the pond, things have been somewhat different. Where, throughout the '70s and '80s, *Playboy* continued to complement erotic content with extensive arts and current-affairs coverage, English publications such as *Mayfair*, *Mensworld* and *Escort* deemed the inclusion of a single article on whisky distillation or white-water rafting cultural edification enough for its readers.

The French take an altogether different approach to the notion of publishing "straight" journalism in a pornographic context. I know because I have just spent a week in La Bibliothèque Pornographique in Lille perusing back issues of the Parisian monthly *Neptune*, published from 1969–78. Like *Mayfair*, *Neptune* tended to annex straight journalism to the final pages. But the similarities end there, for the content is far, far stranger. Not only were authors not restricted to parodically macho themes, but were allowed, it seems, to pick things at random. *Neptune* was clearly a refuge for left-field humorists and wayward academics – all of whom had the balls to write under their real names rather than hiding behind the nom de plume.

The article below, 'Fruit Hosiery', is by none other than Roland Barthes. The translation is my own. I have been as faithful as possible to the original, with one exception: for certain French proper nouns (places and brand names etc.) I have substituted contemporary English equivalents. Some readers may feel that this constitutes a sacrilegious "rewriting" of Barthes's text; I am inclined to think he would have approved of the semiotic slippage arising from substituting one set of signifiers for another.

The other day I bought an apple – I think it may have been a Pink Lady. Let's say it was, for the name is so much more suited to the *thrust* of my story than "Braeburn" or "Granny Smith". Anyway, it was massive, mythically large, this apple: the kind found in fairytales or Genesis 2:16–17. Although I had acquired this apple not from some baleful serpent or wicked witch, but from Costcutter on Kingsland Road in London – and would probably therefore not be suffered to sleep for a thousand years or unwittingly bring about the Fall of Man – I could not deny that its packaging made it far more covetable than any apple I had previously encountered in a retail context. For it was not so much packaged as wearing an all-in-one body sock reminiscent of a fishnet stocking.

Now, I had paid for this apple, so it stood to reason that it was mine to consume. But before consuming it I was evidently obliged, not to unwrap, but to *undress* it, to divest it of the hosiery that the designer of the Pink Lady's outfit had chosen to place between us – the other garments presumably having been discarded as he carried his anthropomorphic project through to its logical conclusion.

And yet the sure knowledge that the Pink Lady would shortly "be mine" was offset by the fact that I had done so little to win her. I had simply handed some coins to a man behind a counter, who immediately relinquished control of the Pink Lady, allowing me to escort her from the premises without so much as a warning as to what might happen if I tried any funny business... *Could* a beauty such as she be so easily won? Surely I was not going to be allowed to go all the way with this remarkable piece of fruit without first jumping through a few romantic hoops? I felt as men feel on visiting a prostitute for the first time. I was overcome by the guilty urge to take the Pink Lady to see a Richard Curtis film, for a pizza in Kettners and a cocktail at the Atlantic. And perhaps, in the small hours of the morning, rather than accepting her invitation to come in for a coffee, I would gallantly decline and return home on the night bus.

The Pink Lady certainly seemed there for the taking, but it occurred to me that there might be a darker story behind this apparent wantonness. Maybe she'd just fled some gentleman's venue, seen too much and been forced to take heel in her underwear to evade a brutal beating at the hands of its unscrupulous proprietor. Perhaps I should not so much *eat* the Pink Lady as drape my jacket around her shoulders and call the police.

But then again…

I sat down on a bench, placed the Pink Lady on my lap and poked the end of my little finger through the stocking. She did not respond to my delicate touch. I then used my right index finger to manipulate her stem while slipping my left beneath her underwear. Something awakened inside her. Emboldened, I shoved a finger into that part at the base of the apple that most resembles an anus, using my thumb to massage what I no less rationally deduced to be its perineum. The Pink Lady gave a murmur of pleasure – faint, it is true, but a murmur nonetheless, and one that to my ears signalled aquiescence. But could I be sure? Perhaps this was not a green light but an amber one: the kind of "yes" that in the confident hands of a determined prosecution counsel would eventually turn out to mean "no". The contract I'd brokered in Costcutter would presumably uphold rather than jeopardize my claims that our intercourse had been consensual, but was I really willing to run the gauntlet of a jury of men and women who might beg to differ?

I decided that I could not possibly take such a risk. I simply couldn't go through with it. I went back into Costcutter. The manager was more than happy to change the Pink Lady for a Granny Smith.

– *Neptune*, 1972 (translated 1997)

The Hudson Variation

The last decade has seen a steady increase in the publication of football-hooligan memoirs. This literary activity has coincided with a decline in football-related violence, but while football hooligans have been trading cudgel for pen, followers of other sports seem to have grown more belligerent. The reputation of rugby, that most brutal of games, remains ironically unblemished (confrontation being lived out vicariously on the pitch), but cricket, hockey, athletics and even indoor bowls have all suffered from crowd violence in recent years. OK, so the recent trouble at Hopton-on-Sea was probably a one-off, the crowd's misbehaviour having been provoked by Karl Power, who invaded the arena dressed as an umpire. Power's sporting situationism – he is best known for gatecrashing Manchester United's pre-match team photo at the 1999 Champions League Final in Munich – has until now been met with guarded admiration. But the indoor-bowls fraternity appears to lend credence to the claim that intolerance increases with age, for the former labourer, having executed his stunt, was lynched by a posse of furious senior citizens.

Prior to this incident, most people would have assumed indoor sports – even the more combative ones

like basketball and ice hockey – to be quite beyond
the stigmatization of crowd violence. I was completely
disabused of this notion on a recent visit to the Chess
& Bridge Shop on Baker Street in London; you might
even say I stumbled upon evidence of a small canon of
literature on the subject. I had revived an adolescent
interest in chess by embarking on a correspondence
match with a friend in Australia, and was having
problems with my opening as black. Having purchased
a pamphlet on the Slav Gambit, I found myself browsing through the second-hand section in search of some
lighter reading to supplement the hard-core analysis
I would be undertaking in the coming months. Chess
literature takes no prisoners, most books assuming a
familiarity with this or that opening, and even those
which offer anecdote and biography are littered with
exhaustive notation. However, I eventually found one
that wasn't, entitled *The Hudson Variation*. I opened it
at the central sequence of photographs, expecting to see
prosaic documentation of tournament play, men facing
each other over spartan tables, flanked by chess clocks
and miniature national flags – and saw images of blood-
ied youths scuffling with stewards in visibility vests,
young men naked from the waist up being frogmarched
out of community centres by policemen…

I'll return to these photographs later, but before I
describe the rest of this book, some facts about its
author. John Hudson has played competitive chess
since 1974, briefly competing as an International Master
(one below Grand Master) in 1982. Though described

in the biography as "a freelance writer since 1987", his corpus is not an extensive one, comprising no more than two dozen articles for such periodicals as *Kingpin*, *Woodpusher* and *BCM*, plus a rebarbative column in the *Sunday Telegraph*. Despite the theme of *The Hudson Variation* and the evident volatility of its author, Hudson is not, and has never been, an actual chess hooligan. His book, like those of many ex-football hooligans, is constructed around the testimonies of others, but his commentary on their exploits is far more academic than we are used to seeing in this genre. For not only are we introduced to all the major firms that followed the teams of the North-West Orbital League during the period 1990–2004, we are also offered a substantive reasoning for their exploits. That said, the author's considerable chess acumen is deployed in unapologetically populist fashion, positional analysis being restricted to the briefest of notations. Hudson is interested less in the positional than in the spectatorial ramifications of a given move; in how incendiary openings like, for example, 1. A4... 2. H4 are, in their voluntary concession of immediate positional advantage, the chess equivalent of "I'm going to beat you with both hands tied behind my back just to prevent me from falling asleep". Noted exponents are compared to footballing counterparts like Vinnie Jones and Jimmy Case, who liked nothing better than to stamp their midfield dominance by committing a bookable offence in the centre circle a few seconds after kick-off.

The contention that such tactics are less intent on victory than on representing the fans' tribal fanaticism on the field of play is qualified with an analysis of several inflammatory openings. As if anticipating our scepticism that latent disquiet can be stoked into full-blown violence simply by pushing a small piece of lathed wood from one square to another, Hudson suggests that another reason for the escalation of the crowd violence first seen in the late Eighties is that chess is essentially boring. That is to say, it has *become* boring. Given the author's professional commitments, this is almost certainly a piece of devil's advocacy designed to get the lay reader's attention. According to several commentators, the game, though far from dead, *is* at a crossroads – a view endorsed by no less a figure than Nigel Short, who stated in a 2005 article in the *Guardian* that he could "foresee a time when it might be necessary to... abandon 'old' chess". While not going quite so far as to favour the adoption of radical "Fischer random chess" (whereby the pieces are shuffled on the back ranks, increasing the potential number of starting positions by a factor of 960), Short implies that the rote learning of positional strategy, revolutionized in the last decade by online databases such as ChessBase, is beginning to stifle inventiveness and could be bad for chess in the long run. Even at intermediate level, little is risked until halfway through a game, white's opening being met with the anticipated black defence. There are exceptions to the rule, but these exceptions are more likely to end in crushing defeat than in a significant contribution to the canon of chess literature. Usually, the openings of the top games appear like rehearsed formalities, with both opponents cracking out the anticipated moves in minutes if not seconds. Even non-chess fans will recall the Short-Kasparov world-title match televised on Channel 4 in 1992. In more or less every game the commentators predicted all the opening moves. "For the uninitiated," writes Hudson, "the action must have had all the appeal of a slow-motion bully-off. At what point, the producer must have wondered, would the action truly begin?" In other words, when would the players' prepared openings and predictive strategy give way to more extemporized play? To chess aficionados such questions will doubtless seem not just naive but against the obdurate spirit of the game. But it's in Hudson's interest to raise them, for it is precisely this obduracy that he suggests fosters an atmosphere conducive to chess violence.

The Hudson Variation is rather slow in delivering the blurb's promised "first-hand account of aggro on the lower tables at Colindale, Brentford and Rick-mansworth", for not until chapter two do we meet any actual exponents of casual violence. By far the archest member of Hudson's ship of lost souls is Captain, founder of the Significant Minority, a Hounslow-based firm active since 1988. Captain is a legendary figure in the North-West Orbital League, credited – even by his adversaries – with bringing the profile of chess violence into line with that of other sports. When police presence at matches increased in the mid-Nineties and the trouble shifted away from actual chess venues to

the surrounding neighbourhoods, Captain's military
acumen was instrumental in scoring a number of remarkable victories for the Significant Minority. And
yet despite his pivotal role, Captain remains a rather
mysterious character, mainly because his exploits are
recounted not by him but by his adjutants. Of these,
George Birch is by far the most eloquent. So much
space is given to Captain's right-hand man that he often
comes across as an author surrogate, the primacy of his
narrative providing such a novelistic feel that the reader
is occasionally reluctant to rejoin Hudson's academic
commentary. Birch's intense loyalty to Captain seems to
stem from an incident in 1989, an incident that sounds
very much like an initiation:

I was fifteen and had travelled to my first away match
in Northwood. I'd planned to go with a school friend,
but a last-minute parental ban meant he hadn't showed at the station. I had misgivings about attending
my first away match alone, and when I arrived at
the Sidney Dye Memorial Hall, penned in with a
raucous crowd of Hounslow West, well, I don't mind
admitting that these misgivings turned to mild panic.
To hear all that obscene and hateful chanting on telly
in the comfort of your own living room is one thing;
to be right next to it is another. Earwigging, I sussed
that the Hounslow boys had travelled to Northwood
early, way before the match, got tanked up, marched
down the Unthank Road and taken Northwood's
boozer, the Needle Gun, without meeting any

serious opposition. Some vicious openings on the lower tables and an unexpected early victory on the top board with the black pieces had only increased their fervour. This rabid band of men, who had probably yet to become known as the Significant Minority, were expressing their disdain for the Northwood following in no uncertain terms, and would probably have attempted to take the opposing end of the Sidney Dye, but it was obviously not enough of a challenge. The rest of the match (drawn 5.5–5.5) passed uneventfully and we filed out of the building, making our way back to the station. I say "we", for I was walking alongside those who'd been seated around me, having been herded outside with them by the stewards. We took a detour through the shopping precinct, where there was more chanting, petty pilfering and random abuse of passers-by, and turned the corner up the hill to the station – only to run into a group of twenty Northwood who'd been informed of the earlier liberties taken and come to the station to bid us farewell. The sight of wrenches, claw hammers and worse confirmed they had no intention of fighting a straightener. Now, I wasn't exactly right *amongst* the Hounslow boys at this point, but I wasn't exactly distancing myself from them either. I was contemplating my options when a voice at the rear consolidated them for me: "*Never* run." These were the first words I heard Captain speak, and when I heard them something told me that running was not an option, and never would be.

The Hounslow boys parted and Captain took his place at the front, let out a roar and... ran – ran *at* them, that is. Northwood's bottle jobs fell away instantly, dropping their weapons and legging it, leaving even numbers tearing into one another. ("The good thing about away matches," Captain was later to remark, "is that bottle jobs don't even get on the train, so you know you can count on everyone who's made the trip. If you've *got* ten, you *are* ten. You get me?") The outcome was a foregone conclusion: we chased them up the Unthank Road, kicked the shite out of them and rubbed salt in the wound by calling in at the Needle Gun for some more refreshment. I had a strange feeling of contentment on the train home. Captain, handing me a take-out, enumerated our achievements: "*Run* 'em, *did* 'em, and took their boozer. *Twice*. Practically un'eard of. Not a bad day's work for ten of us."

A quick count confirmed Captain's gang actually numbered nine. George Birch, Esquire made ten. I was touched.

Thus begins Birch's long-standing association with Captain. Subsequent forays onto enemy soil are recounted with equal relish, and chronicle a swift rise through the ranks from diffident conscript to able lieutenant. As his eventual drill sergeant and sole confidante, Birch is well qualified to fill us in on Captain's early years, which are a parody of institutional neglect. His case is typical: constant domestic unrest, parental discord, divorce and serial remarriage. A successful altercation with a stepfather engenders early feelings of omnipotence. A spree of violent behaviour ensues, culminating in a period of correctional detainment: borstal works its magic, Captain completes his "HND in having it" during a two-stretch in Pentonville for grievous, and by the age of twenty has foresworn all vocational ambition for a life of state subsistence and petty theft.

Captain's firm comprises prison associates, borstal peers and, as Birch's own recruitment testifies, occasional waifs and strays. While many of his infantrymen bear nicknames that are basically onomatopoeic renderings of combat (Tonka, Enoch, Cosh), the most fearsome warriors – and this seems to be the case across the whole spectrum of hard men, from kindergarten tearaway to gangland overlord – tend to retain their full monikers: Mickey Norton, Kev Garrod, John Askew, Ray Leadbetter. There are a surprising number of lone mercenaries, tooled-up maniacs with no specific affiliation: Hatchet Will, Zulu, Mallet. One character is referred to simply as "the beer monster from Friern Barnet", and drifts for years from one firm to another in search of aggro, before finally pledging allegiance to the Significant Minority in a moving ceremony at Scratchwood Services. What unites these men is not some grudge against society (many raise families, pay taxes), just an insatiable appetite for arbitrary one-to-one combat. Tempers are brought synthetically to the boil at the weekend with the electrode of sporting rivalry, but quickly cool once the thirst for violence has been slaked. It's a pastime, a hobby, something to do of a Saturday. Rarely are personal grudges held.

But there are some rivalries that can simmer through the long winter months which invariably separate return matches, and even through the languid caesura of the close season. The Significant Minority enjoy just such a rivalry with the Greenford Martyrs, and the final chapter recounts the bloodiest battles between the two firms. With them it certainly *is* personal. There are several reasons given for this, the most seductive of which justifies the detailed picture of Captain's childhood painted earlier by George Birch. Birch may never actually *state* that Lenny Ripper, the leader of the Greenford Martyrs, is Captain's older half-brother by his mother's first husband, that their feud is motivated not by recreational violence but by a struggle for sovereignty of their mother's affections, but the reader is given ample opportunity to make the inference. Both men appear only once in the photographs which accompany this book – fighting toe-to-toe at an Enfield Lock meet in 1994. Though the picture is too grainy to yield up any striking family resemblance, the aggression it captures certainly seems more than recreational.

Once the novelty of its unusual subject matter had worn off, I found *The Hudson Variation* rather disappointing. The reader waits in vain for Hudson to break off from his steel-toe-cap view of "aggro on the lower tables at Colindale, Brentford and Rickmansworth..." and return to the evident incongruity between chess and violence addressed so manfully in the introduction. But having been dealt with here, it is returned to again only in passing in the remainder of the book. Indeed, the later references to chess are so comically incidental – open the book at any page beyond the second chapter and you are basically reading a generic hooligan memoir – that I fleetingly entertained the notion that *The Hudson Variation* was the result of some publishing farce, whereby the proofs of two very different books from the same publisher became spliced together en route to the typesetters. The seeming oxymoron "chess violence" is really only augmented by the photographs. These seemed to me so convincing that they had to be fake, so I traced them to the various agencies and picture libraries listed in the illustrations, expecting to draw a lot of blanks. All were authentic.

– *Nose Ointment*, 2007

The Okey Cokey

Every other Wednesday I take my nephew to the Juniper and Barnardo Club on Cable Street for an evening of song and dance, a fortnightly revisitation of all those East End classics – 'Roll Out the Barrel', 'Any Old Iron', 'Do What You Do Do Well' – that always ends with that most edifying of spectacles, 'The Okey Cokey'. My nephew's favourite bit is when "you put your whole self in and take your whole self out". I suspect that this is because Uncle Sean, though keen and committed when it comes to putting his whole self *in*, is, if he's being totally honest with himself, a little bit slow at taking it *out* again. His right arm and his left arm, his right leg and his left leg, he can manage pretty well: these he is able to offer and retract with comparative ease, with *almost* as much agility as anyone else. But when it comes to the insertion and retraction of his entire corporeal being, well, no one struggles more than he. And no sooner has he finally contrived to remove his whole "self" from the ring of revelry in the traditional fashion (i.e. by jumping backwards), than the words to the song oblige him to insert and remove it again, double-time, almost at once! With the result that, while the other participants

are going "in-out-in-out, shake-it-all-about", Uncle
Sean has fallen even further behind, is only just
taking his whole self out again; and when, with
excellent slapstick, he has finally executed this almost
impossible manœuvre, this *simultaneous* insertion and
retraction of his entire twenty-stone bulk, and is just
on the point of "shaking it all about", everyone else
is going, "Oooh the okey-cokey-cokey!" and waving
their arms in the air. This spectacle of Uncle Sean
marooned now in the middle and now outside of
the ring, like the ever-excluded single set in a Venn
diagram drawn specifically to illustrate his motor
incoordination, is a delightful one to my nephew,
for it always culminates in Yours Truly singing,
"Knees bent, arms stretched, rah-rah-rah," and
performing the accompanying moves *all on my
own*, in complete silence, the needle catching on the
record's lead-out grooves in mockery of this indefat-
igable soloist.

Heaven forbid that I should ever resolve to master
'The Okey Cokey', for to master it would be to
diminish the achievements of my peers, would be
to imply that *anyone* was capable of doing it – that
no skill or style were necessary. To inflict such a
heresy on the Juniper and Barnardo Club would
be unthinkable, and would rightly result in my
immediate exclusion. And yet, any such success, or
even slight improvement on my part, would already
be *tantamount* to my exclusion, for no longer would
I have a role to play. I would become invisible; we

would *all* become invisible, subsumed into a single unit of tight, flawless choreography. I am determined to prevent that. Determined.

Next week we will look at 'Heads, Shoulders, Knees and Toes'.

— The Hamilton Journal of Contemporary Dance and Physical Theatre, 2001

Austurbaejarbio

Until recently, opinion was divided over whether the term "The Fall" refers to Christian theology, to the English translation of a novel by an unknown twentieth-century author or to a group of cultural freedom fighters whose members spanned three centuries. It is now known that the first two interpretations are false. However, the recent discovery by archaeologists of the fragment known as *Austurbaejarbio* has confirmed that we know even less than we thought about The Fall.

Historians tell us that the achievements attributed to The Fall are the cumulative curriculum vitae of protagonists who lived during the period 1850–2050. Throughout its many incarnations, The Fall has adopted a consistent hierarchy: a team of able lieutenants led by a highly demonstrative captain. The military comparison is apposite, for up to the mid-twentieth century armed struggle was an activity the group returned to time and again. In fact, its founding members were almost certainly professional soldiers. Prior to the publication in 3049 of the initial findings from *Austurbaejarbio*, The Fall's chronology beyond the late 1970s was the subject of dubious speculation. We know that in the preceding decade it had been Leeds United Football Club; that in the immediate post-war period it had been a kosher bakery on Vallance Road in London; while during the Second World War its members – perhaps lacking the galvanizing leadership of a demonstrative captain – dispersed to join a number of militias in offensives both for and against the Allies. In the 1930s it had mounted a series of ambitious civil-aviation initiatives.

We know also that a small infantry of unspecified African nationality calling itself The Fall fought in the 1879 Anglo-Zulu War alongside the Natal Native Contingent. After participating in the successful defence of Rorke's Drift, they mysteriously vanished, only to turn up again in 1881 at the end of the First Boer War – this time fighting against the British at Majuma Hill. A decade later, a group of that same name was said to have exercised remote but decisive influence over the ideology of the Aesthetic Movement. Contrary to widespread belief, it was not the trial of Oscar Wilde that precipitated the end of that movement, but The Fall's assassination attempt on his nemesis, Alfred Lord Douglas. There is a painting by James McNeill Whistler entitled *The Fall* in the National Maritime Museum in Greenwich, thought to be a self-portrait with a group of merchant seamen posing as infamous biblical scapegoats (Adam, Cain, Judas, etc.). But Whistler's diary entries of that time confirm that he had known these sitters for years before he painted them, lending credence to the theory that the picture is not, as historians thought, a modern interpretation of a biblical theme, but a "straight" group portrait of The Fall's captain and his lieutenants – a typically Whistlerian double bluff. It seems that the renowned advocate of "art for art's sake" was not just a nodding acquaintance of the group but its secret impresario.

According to Bertrand Russell's 1935 essay 'The Case for Socialism', in 1900, eschewing an invitation from General Piet Cronje to participate in the Second Boer War, The Fall turned its attention briefly to the livery and visual rhetoric of trade-union politics, producing a number of beautifully embroidered protest banners. The hours expended on these labours not only allowed the group to deploy skills handed down by former members who had trained under William Morris, but afforded the opportunity to discuss ideas that would lead eventually to the formation of an esoteric think tank now acknowledged as an important forerunner to English Vorticism. Thus began an affiliation with early-twentieth-century avant-garde cultural revolt that was to last all through the Great War (which The Fall spent in Zurich, staging rival cabarets to the Dadaists' increasingly bourgeois productions).

Those are the facts that were known prior to the excavation in Reykjavik. It will be noted that what The Fall did in the 1920s is still something of a mystery; until recently, so were its *late*-twentieth-century activities.

The discovery of artefacts bearing information alluding directly to their function is quite rare in archaeology. Amazingly, however, *Austurbaejarbio* contains just such information, included as a supplement printed on paper and folded carefully into its tiny casket. Written in Platonic form, as a dialogue between The Fall's captain and an interlocutor from an organization called the *New Musical Express*, this appendix is far more copious than the fragment itself,[1] and is the only known source of information on the group's late-twentieth-century incarnation. Of all the things gleaned from this dialogue, the news that The Fall spent this period apparently writing "musicals" – a now defunct theatrical form about which little is known – has been greeted with most surprise.

In this interview The Fall's captain is grilled over these musicals and asked to justify them. This he manifestly refuses to do, so their precise nature is never clarified. The Fall's work is described by the gentleman from the *New Musical Express* as "post-punk", "new old wave" and "pre-post-punk"; it is said to be "pop without parameters", "rock without rules", "art without the wank", and to have fostered a form of "degenerate puritanism" impervious to the "sleazy commerce" of the "majors" and their "units" and the "banalizing instincts" of the "A&R man". The group is said to be resistant to "traditional notions of fanbase loyalty"; to have shown their "fans" the "belligerent disdain we all secretly crave from our idols". Reading between the lines of this baffling vernacular, it can be inferred that the musicals listed on *Austurbaejarbio – Hexen Definitive*, *Kicker Conspiracy*, *Oswald Defence Lawyer* and *The*

---

1. The appendix is dated 2008, whereas *Austurbaejarbio* itself is dated 1983.

Man Whose Head Expanded, to name just a few[2] – are apparently a tiny fraction of a great many produced by the group and said to have been preserved on "stereophonic vinyl", "audiotape" and "digital formats". Whether *Austurbaejarbio* is a surviving example of any of these, archaeologists are reluctant to say. The *New Musical Express* implies that they were produced in large quantities, so perhaps they were symbolic "units" of exchange in a bartering system. Precisely *what* they symbolized and what part The Fall's "fans" played in the exchange – i.e. whether the "units" were given to the "fans" by the group, or vice versa – is a secret thought to have died with the maligned "majors", whose ultimate *raison d'être*, as individuals who outranked The Fall's captain, was, it seems, to circulate as many of them as possible. As to the "fans" themselves, while it is clear that what is meant by this term is "people", it is not clear whether these people were actual members of the group or ordinary members of the public. Some have suggested that neither may be the case: that they were to the late-twentieth-century incarnation of The Fall what the British were to its Victorian forerunner, that perverse African infantry at Majuma Hill in 1881; and that the "stereophonic vinyl", "audiotape" and "digital formats"

---

2. A comprehensive list of musicals by The Fall is provided in Margaret Regan's essay 'How I Wrote *Elastic Man*: Musicals, the Enigma of a Forgotten Form', October No. 4291 (3047), pp. 35–59. 'How I Wrote *Elastic Man*' is thought to be The Fall's only attempt to provide a critical framework for the musicals written during this period, which are thought to have differed markedly to those of practitioners such as Andrew Lloyd Webber.

were not benign "units" of exchange but artillery aimed by The Fall at their "fans" – which would explain the "belligerent disdain" that their captain expresses for them in the interview with the *New Musical Express*.

Others have gone further and claimed that there is *no* distinction between the group and its "fans". The evidence for this, they say, can be found in The Fall's recruitment policy during this period, which is glossed in the interview in forensic detail. While, as I have already said, the nature of The Fall's "musicals" is not known, it is clear that their continual staging required a change of personnel unprecedented in the group's history.[3] Where, hitherto, the changes in personnel had been generational, they now increased dramatically in frequency – recruitment and expulsion occurring on an annual basis, often against the will of both the incoming and outgoing members.[4] The nature of the hiring and firing appears to be consistent with that employed by The Fall at its military inception: on the same morning that one member of the group had been released, it was not uncommon for an ordinary member of the public to be served with papers detailing their conscription into The Fall. However, unlike the military – which to this day comprises mainly of the working classes –

3. This in itself is not remarkable: the one thing known about musicals is that they had large casts and ran for many years. In her essay, Regan estimates that "a typical production would employ tens of thousands of people over a thirty-year period" (op. cit., p. 39). From its inception as a musical production company in 1977 to the date of the *New Musical Express* interview in 2008, The Fall got by with just sixty – which is remarkable.

4. The Fall kept the same captain throughout this period.

white-collar workers, company directors and life peers were all as likely to receive written orders to report immediately to a "studio in Salford" and "play bass" on an "album track" as manual labourers and those in receipt of welfare.

Little of this jargon will make sense to present-day readers. Scholars have toiled long and hard in their translations of *Austurbaejarbio*, bringing a cabbalistic fanaticism to their decipherings of its cryptic pronouncements and ideograms. Slowly but surely, they are assembling a picture of the late-twentieth-century "post-punk" musical. However, besides the gnomic character of the actual text – for instance, what is the meaning of the strange upper-case inscription "SOUNDBOARD RECORDING LIVE AT"? – there is also the puzzling question of why it was not written on a more conventional surface, why a shiny silver disc was chosen in preference to papyrus or stone. I wonder, could this be the key to fathoming *Austurbaejarbio*'s meaning?

– Anistoriton, 3051

The Society of Interdependent Artists

Art history abounds with "difficult" exhibitions. The most spectacular conflict of artistic and institutional interests on record is probably Robert Morris's 1971 Tate retrospective, closed after just five days due to health-and-safety concerns – several visitors having injured themselves on the obstacle course the artist had devised as a demonstration of "sculpture in the expanded field". It was in response to the need for such conflicts to be better anticipated that subsequent practitioners evolved a more rigorous critique of the relationship between institution and artist, replacing the somewhat antiquated host-guest model with more innovative approaches. It is within this tradition that I should like to consider the Society of Interdependent Artists' 1995 Exhibition. The Society was founded in 1930 as the Society of *In*dependent Artists, and what follows is, I suppose, the story of how its name came to acquire three more letters.

As with most art "societies", the Society of In(ter)-dependent Artists' annual open-submission show exhibits work by members and non-members. However, *all* members' works are exhibited, for an artist's status as a member of the Society is held to transcend any qualitative judgement that might be brought to bear on his work. While all members have formally to submit works before a judging panel, none is ever rejected, even when his work falls short of the required standard – the only factors ever leading to a member's rejection being death or senility. In the rare though not unheard-of event of an elderly member's paintings being rejected, the Society will often use work from an earlier period to ensure that his inclusion in the show is not a *total* embarrassment. For the most part, though, members continue to produce and exhibit new work well into their nineties, which is why there is so little room for non-members, who alone run the gauntlet of rejection.[1]

Until 1959 the judging panel consisted of twelve members plus the President of the Society, who held a casting vote. A work required ten votes to be accepted. Works that got seven or fewer votes were rejected, while those that garnered eight or nine were held for a second round of judging (more about which in due course). In 1960 the Society adopted the policy of adding a guest judge to invigorate the selection process. Initially, this was either a celebrity patron of the arts or some well-known elder statesman of high culture, but since the late '70s, it has tended to be a much younger artist, critic or curator from the more "contemporary" end of the art spectrum – the aim having been to attract

1. Members outnumber non-members by roughly six to one. All along it has seemed that the only reason for including non-members in the show at all is to pay for it (to the tune of £10 per work). Although members pay an annual subscription, the hanging of their work is guaranteed.

a concomitantly younger generation of artist to submit work for the exhibition. The strategy worked well at first: submission figures from 1976 to 1984 showed an exponential increase, which was indeed down to an injection of new blood. In fact, many of these first-time submitters got work into the show, and some subsequently made successful applications for full membership. In 1985 the judging panel contained a judge under the age of forty for the first time in its history. In 1987 it contained two; in 1989, three.

For some reason – to this day no one knows why – the submission for 1990 plummeted, and in 1991 fell still further. With the recession of 1992, submission numbers reached an all-time low, and the Society made history for a second and then third time when the treasurer reported consecutive financial losses in '93 and '94, the full effect of which was not felt until the following year, when it was realized that the budget could not accommodate a guest selector. This policy, initiated in the Society's halcyon days more through indolent curiosity than genuine desire to foment change, had now established itself as an essential part of the Independents' marketing strategy. In the last fifteen years the guest selectors had done much to expand the submission's demographic, and few had done as much as one Nils Nemmend, whose curatorial celebrity had been instrumental in attracting a record submission in 1989. It was in desperation (and with a touch of that delirious, foolhardy optimism which often accompanies the actions of those whose hand is forced) that the Society turned to him once again; the problem was, Nemmend's star had risen so considerably in the intervening years – had been hoisted, indeed, to such prominent heights that a whole flotilla of lesser movers and shakers now navigated by his shining example – that his fee would have been beyond the Society's means even before its impoverished state. But would not the valiant resuscitation of an ailing institution be remuneration enough for one so professedly idealistic in his curatorial credo? Nemmend, a suspiciously malleable putty in the Society's hands, could not agree more, replying that he would be happy to waive his fee – on condition he be given a bigger say in the selection process and in the hanging of the chosen works. The President of the Society, already enamoured of this talisman of '89, bit his hand off without enquiring what, exactly, Nemmend meant by "a bigger say".

As with so many institutions of its kind, the Society tended to embrace pioneering artistic styles only once they had been drained of all critical imperative, making its annual show a veritable diorama of bygone art frontiersmanship. Surprisingly, though boosting the submission numbers, the influx of younger artists had done little to mitigate this. What had been required was a thoroughgoing transfusion, not just the injection of new blood, but the Society somehow managed to assimilate the youngsters without jettisoning the old guard – and thus without disavowing its Heritage Modernism. Moreover, its tendency to appeal to and recruit new members from undergraduate students,

far from reinvigorating the judging process and cat-
alysing the anticipated renaissance, seems actually to
have consolidated the Society's ossification of once
radical artistic expression: the undergraduate is, after
all, wont to pick an "-ism" and stick with it until
someone points out that he is merely re-enacting history. And re-enactment was what the Society did. It
had announced itself in 1930 with the discovery of
Impressionism. It had amazed itself in 1952 with the
discovery of Fauvism. The 1970s saw the invention
of not just Analytic but *Synthetic* Cubism. Which was
nothing compared to the frankly outré Suprematist
canvases that began appearing circa 1982.

It was clear that, however long it took, the Society
would eventually revisit every major critical and sty-
listic flashpoint in art history. The curator Nils Nemmend gleaned this in an instant, and decided that this
re-enactment of art history could not be allowed to
continue.

The format Nemmend devised to revive the Society
of Independent Artists' annual exhibition was based on
a careful examination of the judging process – which, he
learnt, had become increasingly complex over the years.
You'd think that the selection of works would have been
a simple matter of "yes", "no" and "maybe", with all the
maybes given a second look. And so it was for the first
thirty years of the Society's existence. But as the judges
grew older, their reluctance to admit works became more
steadfast. However, this reluctance was offset by the
knowledge that they had to accept *some* or there would

be no exhibition, and led not to the wholesale rejection of work but to a perpetual suspension of judgement, so that having viewed, say, two thousand works (of which around one hundred would be required to fill that space in the gallery allotted to the non-members), the panel would be surprised to learn that only five had received the thumbs-up and that only seventy had been categorically rejected. The remaining one thousand nine hundred and twenty-five, having received the eight or nine votes that constituted a "maybe", would have to be looked at again. I should point out that the Society actually preferred the designation "doubtful" to "maybe". This is significant, for the panel's acceptance of a work was based not on how much they liked it, but on how *little* they *disliked* it; not on a magnanimous recognition of its merits, but on a grudging tolerance of its faults. This was the most fascinating aspect of the Society, which should by now have recognized that the extremes of rejection and acceptance had only an ancillary part to play in the judging process; of potentially far greater interest was the complexity of the "doubt" that overwhelmed the panel year after year and had each member withholding his judgement to such an extent that it was often necessary to repeat entirely the judging process.

Nemmend perceived that this tendency to express only *equivocal* interest in a given work was not necessarily compromised by the ostensibly *unequivocal* selection of that work for an exhibition, and felt that, with some strategic alterations to the way the submission was processed and the exhibition hung, the panel's doubt could be incorporated into the judging rather than retarding it. While the panel were hardly ever unanimous on which works should be unconditionally accepted (and only marginally less divided on which should be categorically rejected), all judges agreed that some works were better than others – which was something. Moreover, as a safeguard against having to repeat the whole judging process, they had already established (in 1972) a system of grading the doubtfuls into the intermediate categories "doubtful 1", "doubtful 2" and "doubtful 3",[2] enabling the panel to discount immediately the tertiary and secondary doubtfuls rather than having to view them all again to cream off the better works. Did they but know it, the Society had, in so doing, already set one foot on the path subsequently taken by Nemmend.

The system of grading the doubtfuls had initially worked well, allowing the panel to include works not by choosing the most wanted but by eliminating the least wanted. The problem was, this process of elimination, this endless sifting, panning and winnowing, had become so fetishized by the panel as to rival in its protractedness those occasions on which the judging had had to be repeated: when Nemmend first arrived in 1989, the subdivisions of doubtfuls had proliferated

---

2. Once a work had been confirmed "doubtful", it was then judged again to determine precisely *how* doubtful: ten to twelve votes for a "doubtful 1" (i.e. *least* doubtful), eight or nine for a "doubtful 2", and six or seven for a "doubtful 3".

into six, and now stood at an unwieldy eight. Nemmend had a feeling this proliferation might end when the number of subdivisions equalled the number of judges on the panel. But Nemmend, when pointing this out to the judges, suggested they not only anticipate this but go further, "much further", and embrace a system whereby a new subdivision was created for each doubtful work. The puzzled President asked how these works would then be reduced to the required number. It was at this point that Nemmend reminded him of his promise regarding the selection and hanging of the works; in short, he told him that they would *not* be reduced, that it would be his curatorial decree that *no* works would be rejected this year, that the "qualitative denotation" which Nemmend believed the proliferation of doubtfuls already constituted could (and would) embrace *all* works – even the rejected ones. Rather than being rejected or accepted, each work would be given a number that corresponded to the enthusiasm it excited among the judges and which, more importantly, would denote its quality in relation to all other works. In this way Nemmend hoped to deliver an exhibition that did not merely endorse the qualities of the accepted works while dismissing those of the rejected ones, but specified the exact degree of approval the Society wished to bestow on a given work. Each would be judged not only on a "good *enough*" policy, but would also have to find its *exact* place on a "continuum of judgement", occupying a qualitative node and functioning as a bridge between incrementally inferior/superior works. The

President, seeing a flaw in Nemmend's plan, asked him how a judge is supposed to compare two subjectively dissimilar but equally competent works – "say, an academically painted horse with a self-portrait done in the modern style" – without being swayed by a natural inclination for either portraiture (in the modern style) or equestrian art. But Nemmend was as usual one step ahead, and aimed to solve this problem by stipulating a common subject for all submitted works. When asked what this might be, Nemmend proposed that he and the President arrive at one by trawling the archives of past shows and selecting the most recurrent theme.

While they were thus engaged, they ironed out some other problems. Or rather, *Nemmend* ironed out the problem that was the President. Though neoteric in his curatorial approach, there was something contradict-orily old-school about Nemmend – a compelling blend of attributes to find in a human being. The late Brian Clough, probably the most notable example of such a person, was fond of reminding us how he liked to resolve disputes between himself and others by calmly listening to their opinion before telling them that he was right. So it was with Nemmend: we can picture the two men stooped over the light box sorting through slides, Nemmend's ear canted to catch the President's cavilling fatuities, his eyes rolling periodically in gestures of weary rebuttal. The most pressing issue was space. How to fit two thousand works into a gallery big enough for only six hundred was a problem that might have stopped a lesser curator in his tracks; it is a measure of the man that in mulling it over Nemmend established the logistical fulcrum for his whole enterprise. To fit two thousand works into a space big enough for only six hundred it stood to reason that, as well as extending the salon-style hanging system right up to the ceiling and down to the skirting board, the submitted works would have to be smaller than in previous years. But instead of stipulating a *maximum* size, Nemmend saw that the prescription of an *exact* one would further augment the continuum of judgement – for it would enable the Society to grid up the gallery and fix the physical location of each submission in advance. The selected works, instead of being stored somewhere in the interim period between the judging and the exhibition (as was usual), could be judged and hung directly on the wall once their position in the continuum had been established. If, after all works had been hung, the panel then decided to review the position of certain paintings, this would be no problem as their common size would make them all interchangeable. In fact, this interchangeability was the most marketable virtue of Nemmend's system, for the following reason: many judges imputed their reluctance to champion specific works over others to a certainty that they would eventually encounter a similar but *better* picture later on in the judging process. But by the time such a picture turned up, most judges found it impossible to compare it by memory with the earlier picture – which was by now inaccessible, buried beneath five hundred other works. We can begin, then, to see the appeal of a continuum in which every picture was visible, how it might purge a hoary frustration that all judges had felt but had never once vented.

Nemmend wanted the submission, judging and exhibition of works to segue into one another rather than being undertaken as distinct procedures: the way in which the works were judged would have a direct bearing on how they were exhibited. For the first time the Society of Independent Artists' annual exhibition would *embody* the nature of the judging process – whose fairness many artists had bitterly contested when collecting their rejected works. 1995 would mark a watershed in the Society's history: the idea of a *salon des refusés* is of course old, but the idea of integrating it with the *salon* itself is a novel one. The show as Nemmend envisaged it would mix the worst with the best. The viewer would see not only the worst and best works, but how one *got* from the one to the other: how one got from the diabolical to the execrable, from the execrable to the inexcusable, from the inexcusable to the terrible, from the terrible to the bad, from the bad to the merely inept, from the merely inept to the perfectly mediocre, from the perfectly mediocre to the imperfectly mediocre, from the imperfectly mediocre to the plain mediocre, from the plain mediocre to the above average, from the above average to the quite good, from the quite good to the good, from the good to the very good, from the very good to the excellent, from the excellent to the exceptional, from the exceptional to the near-perfect, from the near-perfect to the actually perfect, and from the perfect to the sublime… All this excited the young

– 103 –

curator – and unnerved the President, who had perhaps begun to get wind of Nemmend's intention, which was not so much an exhibition of individual works as the construction of his own meta-work: instead of selecting an elite band of works, a group of Somethings from Everything, Nemmend's curatorial premise was to retain Everything, to emphasize quality not by editing out bad quality but by arranging *all* qualities in spectral relation to one another.

No one had ever articulated to Nemmend what, exactly, the Society of Independent Artists was so independent *of*, but it seemed to him that its reputation was, like that of other societies which run open-submission shows, *wholly dependent* on the existence of a largely unseen – that is to say, rejected – majority. The members deigned annually to rub shoulders with a fraction of this majority – with the lucky 100 non-members who were not rejected – more to emphasize their own pedigree than to acknowledge them as equals. Nemmend placated the increasingly anxious President by persuading him that the Society's reputation could, surely, only be enhanced by rubbing shoulders with this majority in its entirety, including the hitherto disenfranchized rejectees, because it is "better to be seen to triumph over all-comers than over a select few". Nemmend's continuum of *all* works not only reified an implicit interdependency between member and non-member, but modified the connoisseurial conceit of the former ("the triumph of good over bad quality") into an allegory of the latter's disaffection and outsiderness and its possible transcendence ("the long and edifying transition from bad to good"). He did not, of course, inform the President that he intended to follow this modification through to the letter, to the letter*s*, of the Society's name. When Nemmend offered to oversee such mundane exigencies of presentation as labelling, wall graphics and the printing/mail-out of invitations, the Society willingly relinquished these irksome duties to the eager and hands-on curator (though had the offer been declined it would doubtless have been rephrased as a demand). And in fact when, on the afternoon of the opening, the banners went up, hardly anyone noticed that the Society had been covertly relaunched as the Society of In*ter*dependent Artists; those who did kept quiet about the "typographical error" in deference to Nemmend's well-known sensitivity to criticism.

When, a week before the show's opening, everything had finally been carried out to his specifications, Nemmend sat back to reflect on the achievement of processing some 2,173 paintings in a mere three days, every stage of which operation – from submission to judging to hanging – he had overseen with monomaniacal vigilance. While every conceivable objection had been anticipated, we should remember that Nemmend was dealing with an institution whose revisitation of the modern canon was still in its infancy; indeed, was not yet even in sight of such milestones as Abstract Expressionism, still less Pop, Minimalism and the subsequent Conceptualist insurrections of the late 1960s. And as for the idea of "curation as critical intervention", well, the President himself harboured a private disbelief that a curator's duties could encompass anything more radical than dusting a vase. The President's palpable unease had emboldened some of the other judges to venture some misgivings about Nemmend's modus operandi, the most contagious of which was the difficulty of locating stylistically divergent works within such a precise qualitative spectrum. To make it easier for them to do so, Nemmend had had to impose a second constraint on the submissions, adding to his initial stipulation of subject a prescribed style of execution. And so it was that the show he surveyed now, the 65th annual exhibition of the Society of Independent Artists (or rather, the *inaugural* exhibition of the Society of *Inter*dependent Artists), consisted of nothing but tigers depicted in the photo-realist style.

But all was not well with Nils Nemmend. Towards the beginning and end of the continuum, the paintings interacted with one another as he had envisaged, the qualitative difference between each of them being incremental enough to vector a curve of continuous improvement.[3] The problem was the rather boring middle section, the vast plain of mediocrity that stretched between its qualitative outposts. The one thing that Nemmend had failed to legislate for was the reality that most art is neither good nor bad but mediocre, and it was mediocrity that risked turning the

---

3. "Improvement" is not quite the right word. The paintings did not so much improve as redouble their conviction that *painting tigers really really well* matters more than anything else.

smooth and edifying passage from bad to good into an arduous cinder path. The sequence of paintings 300 to 1,800 that should have encompassed "inexcusable" to "exceptional", or at the very worst "bad" to "excellent", actually straddled the categories "perfectly mediocre" to "just above average". The show became mediocre too quickly and remained so for too long, undermining the curatorial dynamic. What was needed, then, was a formal device that appeared to uphold it, a *rhetorical* continuum of improvement transposed onto the actual one.

It was by chance that Nemmend arrived at such a device. While watching the technicians cleaning the glass on the pictures, he noticed that the spray from the dispenser would momentarily occlude the work before the cloth wiped it away, and when he caught himself wishing that some of the pictures could remain occluded he knew he had the solution: the qualitative gradient that levelled out so prematurely could be rhetorically underpinned by glazing each work with glass of varying transparency, this transparency being relative to its position on the continuum. In short, the better a painting was, the more of it Nemmend would allow the viewer to see.

Fine in theory, but exceedingly difficult in practice. Sandblasting was tried first – it being the curatorially preferred, if not the most expedient solution – but it was soon realized that the range of transparency required to make 2,173 sheets of glass more and less visible than one another was beyond even the best technology. After further experimentation Nemmend eventually settled

SEAN ASHTON

on airbrushing, a solution that should really have been arrived at sooner given the Mr Muscle spray dispenser that had inspired this presentational revision, and given also that a spray-gun had clearly been used in so many of the paintings themselves.

At last, two hours before the opening, all the paintings had been returned to their respective positions on the continuum, which had been arranged with the worst works first. No. 1 was a monochrome of lamp black. Nos 2 to 10 were ostensibly identical – save for a subtle difference in paint coverage. Works 10 to 45 bore a more markedly decreasing resemblance to one another. No. 46 – or any of ten adjacent pictures, depending on one's chromatic sensibility – ushered in a hegemony of muddy orange taupe that reigned for some thirty works: No. 68 had, in my opinion, something of the subtlety of an urban dawn, when the rising sun and street lamps contest the sovereignty of the sky. Many people have asked me why Nemmend chose to apply the paint to the glass rather than to the work itself; had they seen Work No. 68, and known, as I did, that beneath the glass lay an *hommage* to a famous work by the revered wildlife artist David Shepherd, they would not find it necessary to ask such a question.[4]

Such, then, was the show's metaphysical appeal. Not until No. 364 were the droplets of paint dispersed enough to reveal a significant amount of the picture. Only with

4. The problem with applying the spray directly to the work's surface was that several pictures had impasto brushwork, which would obviously show through – in a manner perhaps reminiscent of Keith Coventry's all-white representational paintings. Such inadvertent contemporaneity was to be avoided at all costs.

No. 623 could the viewer discern any feline vestiges through the painted glass, and it was this work that seemed to announce an emergence from pictorial oblivion into pictorial sentience. Apparently, certain submissions to the Royal Academy Summer Exhibition are "accepted but not hung"; Nemmend's project featured *accepted* works that were "hung but not seen", works that were accepted as *matter* if not as art: works whose inclusion was, so to speak, of an entirely ontological order, given that they were allowed to occupy the same space as more successful works, but not to command the same degree, or indeed the same kind of attention. And yet they demanded to be acknowledged as a necessary experiential preface to the other works, their sequential proximity to which was their sole redeeming quality. But this quality arguably rivalled the supposedly "better" works, for to view the continuum was to embark on a journey of perpetual anticipation and constant deferral – a journey whose whistle-stops one might have expected to grow longer the more visible the works became. But the reverse was true: the viewer was primed for *what was to come* rather than what he was looking at *now*, the velocity of his appraisal increased by an anticipation of qualitative improvement. Although the "worst" works were effectively presented as "matter", viewers tended to look at them for longer, and even return to these pictures to verify subtle differences in colour and opacity.

Of course, there was a point on the continuum where the comparison of one work with another began to acknowledge – while still resisting – the need for a more conventional appraisal of each painting as an artwork in its own right. Work No. 623, being as it was on the cusp between the visible and non-visible (indicating an emergence from pictorial oblivion into pictorial sentience), was for me the fulcrum of the entire continuum. Even now, I feel a curious reluctance to describe the works that followed, the painstaking ascent into mediocrity, worthiness and beyond. The *knowledge* that the paintings became more visible from this point was somehow more important than an empirical verification of the fact. I only got as far as No. 996, but know of others who managed to complete a full circuit of the gallery before the fire alarm went off and we all had to leave the building. Of this minority, none has ever mentioned, when recalling the 1995 Society of In(ter)dependent Artists' Exhibition, an individual work from the end or even from the middle of the show; in fact to this day the commendation of any *specific* work is as unthinkable as a window cleaner singing the functional praises of any single rung of his ladder. No one – *no one* – can remember what the best and only completely visible work, No. 2,173, looked like or who painted it, so it seems that the continuum's formal rhetoric was forceful enough in the early part of the show to exert its spectral influence on the viewer even when the paintings became more visible in the middle to latter part.

A characteristic of the open-submission show is that each annual incarnation must exorcise the ghost of its predecessor while simultaneously trumpeting the prestige of being the latest in a long and esteemed line. The fire that tore through the Society's 65th annual exhibition, as if in pursuit of the man that had so defamed it, threatened to be not just the latest, but the very last word in the history of the Independents. That this enduring institution rose again the very next year in new, rather more spartan premises in Barnes is a testament to its fraternal cohesion. As for Nemmend, *his* only legacy is the Society's surprising retention of *Inter*dependent in preference to Independent. The name *may* have been allowed to stand as the sign of a lesson learnt the hard way, as a reminder that what doesn't kill you can indeed make you stronger – but is more likely down to Nemmend's having squandered the Society's stationery budget for the next decade on headed note paper, envelopes, compliment slips and rubber stamps bearing his epithetical revision.

– The Plastic Arts, 2001

Whipping Boys

Tempting though it may be to believe that the memoirs of a violent criminal have been strong-armed into print – and let's face it, the accounts of appalling brutality do little to dispel the notion – such instances are rare. The reality is usually that the author, just out of prison, broke and too old to resume his career as an underworld enforcer, has limped cap in hand to the nearest journalist. And the foray into literature is trickier than he imagined. The ghostwriter, seen initially by the former hard man as a mere scrivener, gradually asserts co-authorship, and the book turns out to be not merely "My Story" but "My Story, as told to such-and-such". Only on seeing the book in print does the former hard man realize that his bar-stool narrative has been misrepresented by amateur psychology, that his impressive custodial record has been impugned by bizarre Foucauldian analysis. Recently, Ricky Barnfather was less than pleased to discover that his "inability to express remorse for past crimes manifests itself as a constantly reiterated love for his mother"; while Les Cundy reportedly sent word from Wandsworth that Dr Clive Henderson of UCL would be made to pay with his life for describing his cockney wit as "a form of displaced contrition".

Though we may shudder at the beatings, bludgeon-ings, macerations, ocular bayonetings and methodical corpse disposals of the underworld criminal, let us admit that something in us marvels at the *authorship* of his deeds – at the fact that such acts are attributable to a lone human agency. And yet the memoirs of such men are often underwhelming, not just for literary reasons, but because the authorship of the criminal act eclipses its recounting. Randolph Dunbar's new book addresses this problem by telling the story of organized crime from the perspective of the victim, whose testimony is, on the whole, much more articulate than that of your average enforcer. But here's the catch. Dunbar's collection of case studies is far from being the simple inverse of a criminal memoir. *Whipping Boys* is not simply a cathartic rostrum for victims to condemn violence and the moral turpitude of its perpetrators; it is a survey of individuals who are, quite literally, *asking for it*. Not, I should add, in the sen-se of being psychologically predisposed to victimhood; rather, Dunbar's study is restricted to subjects who covet the trappings of victimhood *without regarding themselves as victims*. Admittedly, a tiny minority have led the kind of lives that have forced them to strike a bargain with violence, to integrate it into their lives, and their condition has developed from there. But in most cases it has undergone no such "natural" incubation, and such commonplace examples as the beaten wife who stands continually by her husband are given a wide berth here in favour of "individuals who forge open compliances with anonymous factions".

But it is more difficult to court the ire of these factions than you would think. The whipping boy is a lover of casual suffering, but your average organized criminal is not always a dispenser of casual violence. In fact, it is rarely casual. After all, he has responsibilities. Usually, he has already done time, and cannot expect to reoffend ad infinitum without jeopardizing his business interests. His violence usually has a function and is often meted out according to a specific code. So our whipping boy, our lover of casual suffering, cannot just present himself for dismemberment; he must *earn* the fury of the en-forcer – by pursuing the same channels as genuine victims. In short, he must give him no alternative. He must prevaricate dangerously with moneylenders, open snooker halls in rough districts to attract extortionists, enter brothels without a penny to his name...

Dunbar's book encompasses all these scenarios and more, and paints a picture that is at once grim and comic. But the humour is less gallows than abattoir; body parts as currency is a recurring theme, for whipping boys have a fixation with corporeal forfeiture that is indexically reciprocated by their creditors' tariff systems:

Surely, I protested, an ear was inadequate compen-sation for the inconvenience I'd caused Mr McManus, especially since I wear my hair long? "At least take a finger," I said. But McManus's man was adamant: digital amputation was reserved exclusively for the relatives of imprisoned grasses, and though Mr McManus did indeed take a dim view of clients defaulting on repayments, in this instance "an ear would do". "An ear in lieu," he added with an impromptu poetic flourish. To make matters worse, McManus's man had left his pruning saw in the car so in the end settled for a lobe, which he spat into a hankie and stuffed into his breast pocket.

Underworld bureaucracy is just one of many problems confronting the whipping boy. Another is the enforcer's tendency to employ hyperbolic figures of speech in the heat of the moment. This can lead to high expectations – and dashed hopes:

> When my assailant said he was going to break my arm in thirty places, my exhilaration was more intense than anything I have experienced before or since. I didn't realize an arm *had* thirty places. You can imagine how deflated I felt when, after bringing my radius down dispassionately over the back of a chair, he just sort of threw me into the corner and disappeared through the fire exit. I felt… short-changed.

More experienced whipping boys know that such hyperbole rarely heralds a proper good hiding, that only some well-timed provocation will encourage the enforcer to make good his promise. Chapter 3, 'Lip', is devoted entirely to such backchat, and abounds with tips on how to make a bad situation a whole lot worse:

Courtney had opened negotiations by claiming to be able to show sixty different ways of breaking a man's arm in a minute. The claim seemed to me implausible.

"Sixty?"

"Sixty – you want to pay up or you want a fucking demonstration?"

"In a minute?"

"In a minute."

"Why the rush? I've got all afternoon."

It was not so much my doubting of his abilities that riled Courtney as the assumption that he too had "all afternoon". The suggestion that a self-employed demander of money with menaces had a more flexible schedule than other, more legitimate financiers was a liberty too far for the big man; the red mist descended, he came at me with his huge hands, and I finally got the kicking I so desperately craved.

But the still more experienced whipping boy recognizes that provocation can also be counterproductive. Dunbar quotes an ancient Phoenician saying: *Those who sail close to the wind often make safe harbour*. Whipping boys would do well to bear in mind that a candidly displayed appetite for brutal punishment sometimes induces a reluctance to mete it out. For such an appetite evinces outright insanity, and outright insanity is, according to the eminent behavioural psychologist, one of the very few things able to appeal to an impoverished moral condition.

In short, then, the whipping boy has his work cut out; moments of triumph are rare, and when they come they are not only savoured but recounted with careful, methodical rigour:

> I awoke disorientated, not knowing where I was or how I'd got there. The lingering odour of chloroform soon jogged my memory, and my abduction returned in a cascade of pungent vignettes: the urinous stench of the gents, the crash of the cubicle door, a gloved hand pressed on my carotid; the gaffer tape, the transit van, the loss of vision…

Where your average enforcer's testimony is, stylistically speaking, no-nonsense (bish-bosh, job done, etc., etc.), your whipping boy's has a tendency to linger on detail, to spin out the tale the better to relive it. One feels that there is a *correct order* in which events must be recounted. Moreover, the whipping boy seems more excited by the contextualization of the violent act – its precise occurrence in space and time – than by the act itself. According to Dunbar, he is "a connoisseur of circumstance, his eagerness to interlace subjective and objective experience bearing the unmistakable stamp of the phenomenologist":

> …They'd left me – not *quite* for dead – in a boy's bedroom, of all places. I knew this immediately, for on a shelf opposite was a Buzz Lightyear clock and numerous injection-moulded plastic toys depicting

characters from *Star Wars: Episode 1 – The Phantom Menace*, together with sporting paraphernalia of various kinds: trophies, a table-tennis bat, boxing gloves, Rollerblades, football boots and, somewhat anachronistically, a pair of Dunlop Greenflash trainers – exactly like the ones I remembered putting on the previous morning – into which, even more incongruously, were stuffed what looked like two prosthetic limbs. Not till I swung off the bed and fell onto my cauterized knees did I recognize these as my lower legs: had I died and gone to heaven or what?!

This is hardly phenomenology as Merleau-Ponty understood it. The manner in which the subject is exteriorized as an inventory of increasingly familiar objects – culminating in the sighting of his legs on a shelf – in fact lampoons the phenomenologist's positing of the self as "being-in-the-world": something "unfamiliar", regarded with bafflement one moment, is the very next found to be an object of the most familiar kind.

Detailed topographical description is a characteristic of most whipping boys' accounts, and it is not surprising to see Dunbar consolidate his thesis around it in a rather dense final chapter. The meticulous descriptions of interiors which so often bracket the violent act, though rarely exteriorizing the subject quite so comically as above, can, he says, be seen as retroactive attempts by the whipping boy to construct a kind of "habitat" around trauma. The whipping boy craves traumatic retribution in an unfamiliar setting, preferably at the hands of an anonymous malefactor. Why? "In order to recollect it," says Dunbar, "and in so doing bring trauma into contact with the familiar."

This sounds opaque at first, but scratch the surface and you realize it's a variation on the Proustian axiom that the self is constituted not through first-hand experience of external phenomena but through the subsequent *recollection* of this phenomena: initial events recede into the past in order to be brought into more intimate contact with the self through recollection. Quoting passages from Beckett's *Molloy*, Dunbar argues that first-hand experience, however mundane, is on some level always "alien" and that there is "nothing more alien than an unforeseen trauma". His consequent assertion is that trauma is somehow the "opposite" of the familiar, and that the whipping boy perceives a strange triumph in reconciling these opposites. This is at the root of his desire to *cause* the trauma, for the whipping boy is better able to control the integration into his psyche of an "authored" trauma than an unforeseen one. Or, to put it plainly: there is a difference between a bad thing happening *to* you and making it happen yourself.

Why the relationship between "authored" and "unforeseen" trauma is not analysed with greater moral purpose – that is to say, with a view towards rehabilitating these individuals – is mystifying, given the author's standing in his field. Like so many "case study" books, *Whipping Boys* seems to fetishize the weirdness of its subjects' conditions, to the extent of celebrating them as individuating characteristics rather than seeing them as afflictions. Such misguided humanism is forgivable only when underpinned by extensive qualification – preferably scientific. One can understand the neuropsychologist Oliver Sacks celebrating Witty Ticcy Ray's extraordinary skill at table tennis and jazz drumming (due apparently to the hand-eye coordination imparted by Tourette's), but it is difficult to see what positive by-products a whipping boy's condition could possibly have. Another criticism is that Dunbar's scholastic analysis is insufficiently integrated into the first-hand accounts that form the basis of each chapter. Most of the interesting ideas come at the end, so the reader has continually to refer back in order to corroborate the author's analysis. *Whipping Boys'* structural imbalance betrays an author who set out to write an unabashedly populist work and then fell back on his academic credentials at the last minute. Bookshop managers will have fun deciding whether to shelve it with the hard-man and hooligan memoirs or with the left-field academic crackpots. It may be possible to please the latter and still appeal to the disinterested consumer of casual violence, but not with a book like this.

– Nose Ointment, 1998

Songs of Praise Interactive

I see that Andrew Barr's historical account of *Songs of Praise* (www.bbc.co.uk/songsofpraise) has not been updated since 2008. This is surprising, given the recent resurgence of interest in religious broadcasting, which threatens to become a national obsession in the wake of the BBC's introduction of its *Songs of Praise* interactive package.

Since Tessa Jowell, the Secretary of State for Culture, Media and Sport, brought forward the date for switching off analogue broadcasting signals from 2012 to 2010 – consigning us, for better or worse, into digital perpetuity – nearly everyone has taken advantage of that little red button in some shape or form. However, along with *Crawshaw's Watercolour Cruise* and *Taggart*, *Songs of Praise* is one of the last programmes to go interactive. Now that it has, ratings have recovered substantially, and producers must surely regret not grasping the nettle sooner – especially in light of ITV's phenomenally successful relaunching of *Highway*, its sometime and current rival, reinstated after a seventeen-year absence. The second incarnation of *Highway* hit the ground running in 2009, offering not just the standard bolt-on interactive services but innovations borrowed from reality-TV formats, and it was surprising that it took *Songs of Praise* so long to respond to the new competition. Most commentators ascribe this to complacency, but in some quarters there is a feeling that the inertia was down to the then Director General and former *Songs of Praise* presenter Alan Titchmarsh, who was said to be resistant to the notion of "fixing what ain't broke", and in favour of a return to Reithian values.

Given the durability of *Songs of Praise* – which this year celebrates its fiftieth anniversary – this resistance to change is understandable. However, the current makeover is merely a consolidation of a general transformation that has been taking place since the late 1990s; moreover, it is congruent with the pioneering nature of the programme's inception, which, as Andrew Barr here reminds us, was more impromptu – one might even say "experimental" – than most people imagine:

...one Sunday lunchtime in 1961, Donald Baverstock, a famous producer on the news magazine *Tonight*, watched by chance a test transmission of an outside broadcast of hymn-singing in Welsh from a Welsh chapel. He found it such a compelling experience, wide shots of a beautiful chapel and close-ups of people's faces singing with deep faith, that he suggested to Stuart Hood, then Director of BBC TV programmes, that a programme in English might be just as popular. The Head of Religious Broadcasting was appalled: how could you attract young people to religion with a programme of hymn-singing in church?

This last question was evidently one that Baverstock avoided, for the programme's format – "wide shots of a beautiful chapel and close-ups of people's faces singing with deep faith" – was to remain unchanged until the late 1970s, when "an increased budget meant that instead of simple introductions to each hymn recorded in the featured church, members of the local community now chose and introduced the hymns themselves, in filmed interviews". Baverstock's successors were thus able to be more innovative with the links between the programme's segments, obviating the need for the somewhat pious "disembodied commentary" so characteristic of mid-twentieth-century broadcasting (and now, it seems, heard only in coverage of Remembrance Sunday).

However, just when producers were learning how to exploit the levity of this new feature, along came *Highway*. Presented by comic legend Sir Harry Secombe, *Highway* had levity in spades. When it was launched by ITV in 1983 – ending the BBC's twenty-year monopoly of the 6.15 Sunday evening slot – channel-hoppers could hardly fail to notice that, compared with Secombe's charisma and avuncularity, *Songs of Praise* seemed impersonal, detached and above all, sedentary. As though consciously emphasizing this last aspect, ITV furnished their presenter with a van, enabling him to get out and about and take religion to the people. Viewers of the BBC programme were invited to sit on hard benches in cold medieval buildings and pray for their souls, presided over by an inscrutable parson; viewers of *Highway* were invited to jump in Harry's Ford Transit and shoot the religious breeze as he gunned it up the A10 to a multi-denominational meeting in Cambridgeshire. What's more, while talking about his faith, Harry would occasionally let slip some anecdote about working with Spike Milligan or Peter Sellers. Here was a man with whom viewers might feel *naturally* compelled to sing for their supper – and for no other reason than that they wanted to. *Songs of Praise* was inveterately church-based, the congregation's eyes fixed complacently heavenwards in a state of passive supplication, whereas *Highway*'s proactive peregrinations emphasized the *journey towards* spiritual enlightenment. And here was Sir Harry, a former star of *The Goon Show*, to lead us on that journey, to check our spiritual oil and tyre pressure and entertain us in the many theological service stations we would have to stop at on our path to righteousness.

Songs of Praise later drafted in Dame Thora Hird, who, as a veteran stage and television actress of national treasure status, provided an interesting counterpoint to Harry (with whom she was later to collaborate on *Sunday Morning With Secombe*). However, Dame Thora seemed too... well, a little too *at home* – whereas *Highway*'s appeal lay in the apparent incongruity between its presenter's former status as a pioneer of deeply absurd comedy and his current stewardship of a mainstream ecumenical vehicle. For many, this incongruity held greater fascination than the actual content of this vehicle. As a programme, *Highway* had what TV producers dream of: an appeal that was not intrinsically related to its content.

This is surely an important factor when considering how to seduce the *non*-religious viewing public, for judging by the newly revised formats of the competing flagship programmes it is this secular demographic that preoccupies ITV and BBC commissioners. So what can we atheists and agnostics expect to find on pressing our red buttons on Sunday evenings at 6.15? How are producers catering for *our* spiritual needs? Well, ITV has undoubtedly stolen a march on the BBC by recruiting the atheist prophet Richard Dawkins. Dawkins is allowed to pursue whatever agenda he likes in his explosive inserts – under the (contractual) understanding that he has no control over how his words will be used. It's gradually becoming apparent that the author of *The God Delusion* is being groomed as a rhetorical "Saul" – though quite how producers intend to expedite his conversion on the road to Damascus is as yet uncertain. Nevertheless, Dawkins's anti-religious diatribes have already been deployed in cunningly homeopathic fashion, carefully edited and repackaged as the vitriol of a mercenary academic making hay while the post-9/11 apocalyptic sun shines – with the result that secular viewers are manipulated into throwing their emotional loyalties behind the Church.

But don't write off *Songs of Praise* just yet, for it has recruited a creationist counterpart to *Highway*'s Dawkins, a religious maniac named Mr Bennett who does skits between hymns. "What," I can hear you saying, "surely not the same Mr Bennett from the 1980s children's art programme *Take Hart*, the sinister janitor who supplied slapstick interludes (falling off ladders and looking through inky telescopes) while the programme's eponymous star, Tony Hart, put the finishing touches to, say, a pastel drawing of a Boeing 747 cockpit?" Yes, it is he. And what's more he doesn't seem to have changed much. He has aged, of course, and his living circumstances have clearly worsened, but his psychosis – that of a man whose attempts to break into mainstream TV are rewarded only with those parts that befit the mindset of a man who is "trying to break into mainstream TV", a psychosis that is its own cause and effect, as psychoses tend to be – has survived intact. We are given to understand that it is precisely the aforementioned marginalization that has fostered the bitter compulsion to become a self-appointed emissary of a vengeful God – and given to understand that his role on *Songs of Praise* represents his psychosis in its terminal phase.

So, Mr Bennett is one of those street preachers who tell us that we will go to hell if we don't let Jesus into our lives immediately. He accosts anyone wearing jeans or a leather jacket or carrying shopping bags or wearing an iPod, castigating their blatant ungodliness, building slowly into a tempest of bowdlerized chapter and verse, foaming with garrulous intensity from an imaginary pulpit. He yells at individuals through a megaphone, asking passers-by to "look upon this wretched avatar of Lucifer and note how meekly he stumbles to eternal damnation, oblivious to the certainty of imminent apocalypse, when every *mountain* and *ISLAND* shall be moved from its place." The running joke is that the citizen at whom he has aimed these fulminations removes his baseball cap and sunglasses to reveal that he is none other than Jonathan Edwards, the presenter of *Songs of Praise*. Edwards, the 2000 Olympic Triple Jump Champion and world-record-holder, shakes his head at Mr Bennett and fixes him with a quizzical look, before turning to camera and setting the viewer straight on a few things, quipping that no, he had *not* been offended at Mr Bennett's describing him as "meek", since, as Jesus said, it is the meek who "will inherit the land".

By pressing the red button and following the prompts, viewers can freeze Mr Bennett in mid-astonishment and watch Edwards – whose heel-strike velocity in the hop phase of his 1995 world-record leap in Gothenburg was actually *slower* than that of the second- and third-placed contestants, enabling him to maintain better form through the skip-and-jump phases – move slowly around him, while explaining that the Bible's language is largely symbolic and not to be transposed directly onto our daily lives. Press the green button and his colleague Sally Magnusson will appear in a shimmer of CGI and ask viewers whether they spotted Mr Bennett's misquotation of Revelations, chapter 6, verse 14. Press it again and we're back with Jonathan, who guides us through the rest of the beatitudes, the theological backbone of the Gospel according to St Matthew. The beatitudes scroll across the bottom of the screen in copperplate gothic light. As the fourth beatitude – "Blessed are those who hunger and thirst for righteousness, for they shall be satisfied" – scrolls across, Edwards quips that "perhaps Mr Bennett has taken this one too much to heart", before continuing on to the fifth, sixth, seventh and eighth beatitudes and asking us to consider the Sermon on the Mount within a wider, more contemporary context.

Essentially, then, the BBC is using its interactive service to correct the theological blunders of its janitor turned religious pedagogue, using his fire and brimstone as a prompt for a more balanced textual analysis that is so interesting that one could be watching a literary programme rather than a religious one. This is a highly commendable approach – especially when we consider that Jonathan Edwards, the man to whom it falls to correct these errors, is now fronting *Songs of Praise* as an apostate Christian, having left the show in 2007 after suffering a crisis of faith. Tempted back by the BBC after a four-year absence, the former athlete's extensive knowledge of and enthusiasm for the Scriptures will appeal to all those non-religious viewers for whom they remain an unparalleled anthology of stories. Expect ratings to soar.

Unsurprisingly, ITV has opted for a less canonical approach, using *its* interactive service to explore tensions between the religious and the secular. In last week's programme *Highway* travelled to the Church of St Mary in Sporle, a small village near Swaffham in Norfolk, where there has been a long-running dispute between the congregation and the local football team. Sporle FC, who use a pitch adjacent to the church, insist on playing their matches on Sundays at 11.00 a.m., which coincides with the morning service. This means that Reverend Humphreys's sermons are peppered with shouts of "Man on!", "Square!", "Goalside!", "Re-*ef*!" and "Back and face, back and face!" – all heard against a background of familiar Anglo-Saxon colloquialisms. It is the latter expletives that the congregation is most concerned about. Despite being asked to moderate their language countless times in the local parish magazine, players remain inclined to forget themselves in the heat of battle – and many games do end in fights. Last week, by pressing the red button on their handsets, viewers of *Highway* could have witnessed a fifteen-man brawl on one side of the screen and, on the other, an invitation from Reverend Humphreys to his congregation to advance towards the altar to take Holy Communion.

Highway's producers are clearly fixated by the notion of *concurrence*, for most of their interactive options allow viewers to juxtapose whichever religious service is being covered with "secular" events happening elsewhere in the parish at the same time. Such is the nature of the activities chosen by *Highway*'s provocative producers (glue-sniffing, teenage sex and animal torture are some of the more transgressive), that the General Synod has condemned these tactics as a childish interpretation of the "how can there be a God if bad things happen" principle. Atheists have replied in their usual vindictive fashion. And so it has fallen to the agnostics (i.e. lapsed atheists) to provide the voice of moderation: they point out that the theme of concurrence – the concurrence of religious and secular, spiritual and concrete, miraculous and commonplace – has inspired some of our greatest art. They probably have in mind Auden's famous poem, 'Musée des Beaux Arts', which reminds us that the profound – for instance human suffering and religious miracles – must occur in direct proximity to the quotidian. One of the examples Auden supplies is a torturer's horse scratching its arse on a tree while someone is being martyred. It's a salient image, and the pictures recently broadcast by ITV appear to be driving at something similar, though in a more inflammatory way.

– *TV Quick*, 2011

Causality

In the autumn of 2006 I received an unexpected phone call. I was so used to dealing with tabloid middlemen and gossip-mongers that when my interlocutor introduced himself as the editor-in-chief of *Radical Philosopher* and said that he wished to engage my services, well, I don't mind admitting that the receiver quite literally shook in my hand: here, finally, was an opportunity to show that I too could punch above my journalistic weight. However, as he fleshed out the details I realized he'd made a mistake. "Sorry to disappoint you," I said, "but I believe you're confusing me with *Steve* Ashton, the academic and cultural historian. It happens all the time. You're talking to *Sean* Ashton, journalist, broadcaster, TV panellist and official biographer of Trudie Goodwin, aka Sergeant June Ackland off *The Bill*." To my amazement the editor replied that he knew full well who he was talking to, that he admired my appearances on *They Think It's All Over* and *Children in Need*, and wished to hire me as "a voice of the common man".

He explained that *Radical Philosopher* was commissioning five "non-philosophers" to write an article on a different philosophical theme. Before I could interrupt again, he assured me that each of these non-philosophers

was to be assigned a "mentor", a long-serving member
of the journal's editorial team who would ensure that we
kept within the parameters of the idea to be elucidated.
Our job was simply to "make this idea accessible to
laymen of average intelligence, in whatever way you see
fit". He added that the articles were to be published as a
supplement to *The Mail on Sunday* in an effort to reach
a new audience. It happened that a month earlier I had
been released from my position at *TV Quick*, so you
can imagine that I was relieved at this offer of work,
however daunting the assignment might be.

The following day, the fax machine disgorged the
details of my mission. I had been allocated the theme
of "Causality". I was a little disappointed at first, and
phoned round to ask what themes the other non-
philosophers – all of whom I knew – had been assigned.
Claire (Rayner, that is, the revered agony aunt and
social commentator) had landed "Ethics", which was
understandable. Justin (Toper, the astrologer for the
Daily Express) had been given the ostensibly trickier
task of explaining "Ataraxia". Meg (Matthews, ex-
wife of Oasis star Noel Gallagher and a one-time
colleague of mine at *Take a Break*) had been allocated
"Haecceity". Keith (Chegwin, no introduction needed)
got "Teleology". All in all, I hadn't come off too badly.

Meg had definitely drawn the short straw. But she
had already pledged her fee to charity, so there was
no backing out now – despite her inability to even
pronounce the word "Haecceity" (indeed, none of us

could pronounce it). And Claire's task would be no cakewalk either, despite her formidable experience of affairs of the heart. As an agony aunt, she was used to tackling ethics from the viewpoint of the particular, but could her analysis encompass the generalities that most philosophers seem to deal in? In my opinion the jury was out. Justin, I felt, had the easiest task. I was struck by the similarity in tone between the entry for Ataraxia in Ted Honderich's *The Oxford Companion to Philosophy* and the stock-in-trade mysticisms of the tabloid astrologer: "Freedom from trouble or anxiety..." etc., etc. And then there was Keith. Doubtless gunge tanks, pratfalls, doorstepping and possible nudity would constitute the greater part of his methodology. No, Keith would be all right. Things always turned out all right for Keith, one of life's natural data-gatherers.

As for my own assignment, I soon realized that my confidence was a front, a displaced sense of relief at the fact that I hadn't drawn "Haecceity". This confidence evaporated as, the following afternoon, I sat down to write my treatise on Causality. I'd spent the morning leafing through Honderich's book, but had written nothing. Come to think of it, I'd not even turned my computer on since leaving *TV Quick*, and I noticed that a draft of the article I'd been writing on the day of my departure was still on my desk.

I dozed off around three, and on waking the first thing I saw was a word from the title of this unfinished piece. For a moment I thought this word was "Causality", and that I had somehow completed my assignment in my sleep, or that someone else – my mentor? – had crept in and written the article for me. Then I saw that the word was "Casualty", or, to be precise, *Casualty*, the ITV medical drama series of that name – and a near anagram of "Causality". I recalled what the editor of *Radical Philosopher* had said: "…in whatever way you see fit".

I turned on my computer, created a new document and began typing immediately.

Causality

Episode One: A Breach in the Field of Exceptionless Regularity

Cast:

John Hobbes played by Charles Dance
Jack Critchell played by Gerard Kearns
George Glover played by Jack Davenport
Butler played by Robert Powell

We join the action – set in post-Victorian England – as our causal paramedics speed towards an incident at Watlington Hall, home of radical amateur empiricist Sir Geoffrey Boyson, staunch Humean and controversial advocate of the vertical burial. John Hobbes and Jack Critchell are thrown around the interior of their customized hansom as it hurtles through the night, Critchell assembling equipment, Hobbes leafing manically through a thick volume of maxims, half-moon spectacles a-dangle…

HOBBES: I've got a bad feeling about this one Jack.

CRITCHELL: Me too, John. You see the look on that valet's face?

HOBBES: I'd say that was the look of a man who'd just witnessed an effect without a cause.

CRITCHELL: Or a cause that did not produce the anticipated effect. Recasting paradigmatic singular causes as paradigmatic *general* causes is a Procrustean enterprise, John.

HOBBES: It's playing with fire and no mistake, Jack. Have you prepared Aristotle's Quartet?

CRITCHELL: Well, it's not been touched since we attended that demonstration of Davidson's Proof in Mildenhall.

HOBBES: But you've ensured the four causal paradigms are in working order?

CRITCHELL: John, how long have you known me? Yes, the phials are intact. (*Shaking a flask labelled "The Cement of the Universe"*) The empirical reagent's a bit low, but that can't be helped, as you and I both know.

HOBBES: Damn these government cutbacks, Jack.

Cut to an aerial establishing shot of Watlington Hall, lashed by wind and rain, lightning illuminating the gargoyled battlements, with the hansom just coming into view. Critchell and Hobbes tumble out of the cab before it comes to a standstill, clutching a bewildering array of paraphernalia. They are met by a butler at the door and taken into the billiards room, where they find someone already in attendance...

HOBBES: I might've known: George Glover.

A rakish gentleman in a cape is bent over the billiard table, on which is scattered a number of items: callipers, charts, a tape measure, a pencil and a silver pocket watch. Glover is rolling a ball back and forth across the table insouciantly. He has his back to Hobbes, and speaks without turning his head.

GLOVER: Don't look so surprised, John. I'm Sir Geoffrey's private empiricist, as you well know.

HOBBES: So what the hell are *we* doing here?

GLOVER: It seems Sir Geoffrey's valet panicked. I don't know why; I'm pretty sure all this is nothing more than a case of misconstrued temporality – at the very worst a touch of downwards causation.

HOBBES: What makes you so confident?

– 138 –

GLOVER: Steady on John. You're not addressing one of your apprentices now.

HOBBES: Just give me the facts, Glover.

GLOVER: Well, Sir Geoffrey and Lord Chellingham had just adjourned to the billiards room—

HOBBES: Time?

GLOVER: Just after midnight. Anyway, Chellingham broke off; they were five minutes into the frame when the valet, who had gone over to the sideboard to pour the whisky, looked up to see both men standing motionless, Chellingham in an upright position over there (*gestures towards a chair in the corner*) and Sir Geoffrey bent over the table here (*takes a cue and assumes the finishing position of a player down on his shot*).

HOBBES: So, the valet had his back to the game when the incident – if we may call it that – occurred.

GLOVER: That's correct.

HOBBES: And what, exactly, occurred?

GLOVER: Why, is it not plain man? Have you eyes? Observe the ball.

SEAN ASHTON

CRITCHELL: (*Walks over to the table*) Interesting. John, the cue ball appears to be levitating of its own volition three feet from the surface of the table.

HOBBES: Jack, have I not warned you before of the perils of attributing volition to inanimate matter?

CRITCHELL: I don't believe so, John.

HOBBES: Then consider yourself warned. Carry on, Glover.

GLOVER: Sir John's cue ball – struck with considerable force and heavy topspin – hit the red ball, which you would have expected to be propelled into the baulk area of the table. But the red ball did not move. Furthermore, the cue ball, meeting complete resistance to its kinetic energy where it might have expected immediate transfer, went into the air and has remained in the present position for over two hours.

HOBBES: Hmm. And there's no evidence the red ball was tampered with? Fixed from below, say?

CRITCHELL: I think we can rule out legerdemain, John; I've made a thorough examination.

HOBBES: Thanks Jack. Glover, let me ask you just one question: How do you *know* all this if the valet... what's his name?

GLOVER: Thirlwell, or Wellthirl – something like that.

HOBBES: How do you know all this if the valet fled?

GLOVER: The kitchen maid also witnessed the incident – or its aftermath. On hearing the valet's cries she came down. He told her what'd happened.

HOBBES: So, we have things not from the horse's mouth, but from the groom's, if I may put it like that.

GLOVER: You may put it as pompously as you please, John.

HOBBES: And the butler? (*Rounding, as if suddenly noticing the presence of the fourth man*) Where were you, sir?

BUTLER: (*Coughs, pauses for thought*) I believe I was fetching Sir Geoffrey's cigar-cutter from the drawing room.

HOBBES: So you and the valet were not present in the room at the same time?

BUTLER: As I left the room to fetch the object in question, I was under the impression that the Thirlwell gentleman had just been dismissed for the evening, sir. Indeed, I was surprised, on my return, to find him loitering in the hall wearing his overcoat.

HOBBES: Evidently you ran into Wellthirl just before he left to fetch us. He did not impart his story to you when you met him in the hall?

BUTLER: He said nothing, though his countenance and general demeanour, if I may be permitted the metaphor, spoke volumes. (*Gesturing towards the hovering billiard ball*) I now understand why.

HOBBES: So this is the first you've heard or seen of the matter. Critchell, run some tests on that red ball.

CRITCHELL: Will do, John (*Inserts red ball into a device housed within his folding briefcase*).

GLOVER: Still playing with your toys, I see, John. You really suppose mental-to-physical causation can be detected with such gimmickry?

HOBBES: Let the boy do his work, Glover.

GLOVER: There's no "work" to be done, John. The problem can be addressed in purely metaphysical—

CRITCHELL: On the contrary, Dr Glover, the readings from my instruments disprove your earlier mooted theories of "downwards causation". John, I believe we're looking at a genuine absence of causal necessity here. As Hume says, events during which "…an object, followed by another similar object, and where all other objects similar to the first are followed by objects similar to the second", are not necessarily, in themselves, adequate proof of *universal causal necessity*, but are merely a demonstration of an *exceptionless regularity*. That the regularity of events has, up to the *present* time, unfolded as anticipated, *without exception*, does not logically preclude such exceptions from occurring at any given *future* moment. That the occasion of billiard ball A striking billiard ball B has always been seen to be succeeded by the movement of billiard ball B does not preclude the possibility of billiard ball A striking billiard B one day and meeting complete resistance. What we have here is a breach in the field of exceptionless regularity.

HOBBES: If I understand you correctly John – and I freely admit there's a chance in a million that I do – then there's not a moment to be lost. If this conundrum is to be solved rationally, that is to say, with recourse to logical premises that yield to genuinely analytic interrogation rather than the bogus, shape-shifting metaphysics favoured by our friend Dr Glover here, then we need subjects who are able to recount clearly the teleological lineaments of this seemingly autonomous levitation of a given quantity of spherically arranged matter during an otherwise incident-free game of billiards. But it appears that the participants in this post-prandial folly are not just our only witnesses to the event but its very axes of cause and effect. Unfortunately,

Mr Cause and Mr Effect have fled into the night. We must find them – and fast.

CRITCHELL: John, by all that, can you possibly mean "go out into the garden and look for Sir Geoffrey and Lord Chellingham"?

HOBBES: Jack, that's e*xactly* what I mean. Take as many staff as you can muster. Check the stables and out-houses.

CRITCHELL: (*Moving quickly towards door*) John, I'm already searching those stables and outhouses.

HOBBES: Oh, and Jack?

CRITCHELL: John?

HOBBES: Be careful.

CRITCHELL: Will do, John.

Cue music. Roll credits. A BBC continuity announcer urges us to tune in tomorrow for the second instalment of this two-part drama.

– *Radical Philosopher* in *The Mail on Sunday*, 2011

Conscious Fiction

Richard Wentworth once noted that the art gallery is somewhere between a library and a shop. *Precisely* where depends on whether you're buying, selling or have just come to view the show. Or in my case *re*view the show. I've come to the Eagle Gallery in Clerkenwell to review *Conscious Fiction*, a group show inspired by Merlin James's text of the same name. I've been looking forward to this; recently laid low by a virus, I had not clambered out of bed for two weeks until yesterday, and this was to be my way of easing myself back into work. What could be more revitalizing for the ailing critic than an exhibition of work by ambitious young artists with a reputation to make, a career to hone?

Alas, my convalescence is to be denied the rejuvenating tonic that these four painters would undoubtedly have provided, for a note taped to the door says the gallery is closed for three days: the proprietors have gone to the Islington Art Fair. I suspect I am not the only one to have schlepped the length of Farringdon Road this afternoon, only to discover that the show is viewable not, as the *London Gallery Guide* maintains, from "Wed–Fri, 11–6 p.m. and Sat, 11–4 p.m.", but "by appointment only" for the next three days. We are expected, one feels, to overlook these little mishaps, to forgive the oversights of gallerists who neglect to consult their diaries and arrange the necessary invigilatory cover, or who, on especially quiet afternoons, close up a whole hour earlier than advertised in *Time Out* to make it home for *Star Trek: Deep Space Nine*. The Eagle Gallery's excuse of art-fair priorities somehow just makes things worse, drawing a veil of aspirant professionalism over the amateurish prosecution of its less glamorous duties. But it is the very neglect of these duties that gives the game away: how well can a gallery be doing if it has to close for an art fair? "Maybe you should have phoned," I can hear the reader saying. Maybe I should have. Maybe I should telephone Mr J.S. Sainsbury the next time I want to go shopping: "Good afternoon, this is Sean Ashton here. Yes, the writer and broadcaster. Listen, I need to buy some comestibles and cleaning products and was wondering whether you were planning on opening up today. You are? Capital."

Tonight I fly to Germany for a conference at the Hamburger Kunsthalle, and this afternoon is the only chance I have to see this show. I've heard a lot about these painters, but have seen little or nothing of their work. Is little or nothing enough to review it? It's going to have to be, for my protests to my editor that I can't very well review a show without first seeing it have fallen on deaf ears: "Can't you?" challenged Mr Whitstable. "Can't you? Been done before. Many times, I dare say. If they can't keep office hours that's their lookout. Review the bastard anyway." Let me apologize in advance, then, to James Fisher, Amanda Thesiger, Rebecca Sitar and Orsina Sforza for what I am about to write, for my editor seems to have decided that the gallery you have entrusted with your immediate career prospects needs to be apprised of the consequences of proprietary negligence.

Conscious Fiction presents four artists whose practices share affinities in the deployment of an individual painterly vocabulary to make images which contain resonant, sometimes unsettling ambiguities. It takes its title from a text by the painter Merlin James in which he curated a hypothetical show to test the possibilities and limitations of painting within current visual practice. Limitation is acknowledged in each of the artist's work, whether it be in the non-narrative abstraction of Amanda Thesiger's amorphic forms, or Orsina Sforza's unidentifiable "presences" – that are simply the result of pulsating, fluid sweeps of oil paint on paper. In the works of James Fisher and Rebecca Sitar, which tend towards incorporating elements that can be read more figuratively, any single reading of the image is disrupted by the artists' play with two-dimensional pictorial space and many-layered surfaces of pattern and veils of paint...

No. That just won't do. Any fool can see that the author – perhaps with one eye already on Hamburg – has just copied the press release from the Internet and passed it off as his own work while stalling for time trying to come up with something more interesting to justify reviewing a show he hasn't in fact seen, which would seem arrogant, contemptuous and even baleful were it not for the moral high ground he has already claimed by laying the blame for this state of affairs firmly at the door of the Eagle Gallery – which, let's remind ourselves, was closed. It's the kind of trick one might get away with in *Metro* or *Hot Tickets*, but Whitstable will spot it a mile off. Still, it's taken a sizeable chunk out of the 2,000-word piece he was promised. As for the rest of it, short of hiring a cherry-picker and peering in through the first-floor windows of the gallery, what are we to do?

Our exit strategy from this review must be an extrapolation of what we already know: we will infer from the Eagle Gallery's locked door that *Conscious Fiction* has *never* opened; that visitors have been *intentionally* thwarted in their desire to see the exhibition; that the work alluded to in the press release is *not* hanging in the Eagle Gallery as we speak; that it has *never* existed, and that, furthermore, James Fisher, Rebecca Sitar, Orsina Sforza and Amanda Thesiger are ciphers plucked from nowhere by Merlin James to further reify his factitious conceit. We will assert that *Conscious Fiction* restricts itself solely to themes of closure and inaccessibility, arguing for its inclusion in a genre inaugurated by Robert Barry's 1969 show at the Art & Project Gallery in Amsterdam, for which the artist locked the door and nailed an announcement to it reading "For the duration of the exhibition the gallery will be closed". We will assert that our failure to enter the Eagle Gallery and view the "exhibits" is not the result of mismanagement but a deliberate curatorial strategy. Asked to substantiate this, we will call upon the testimonies of others who have attempted to enter the gallery these last two weeks, only to be met with rebuffs and diversions so various as to invite the contention that here, finally, is an exhibition that, instead of presenting closure as a single monumental gesture (like Barry), offers a series (one might almost say "anthology") of temporary closures caused by unforeseen and mysterious contingencies, seeming, thereby, to lend the theme as many guises as there are viewers. We may even allow the reader to infer that *Conscious Fiction* modifies the facile truism "Beauty is in the eye of the beholder" into "Content lies in the frustration of the thwarted". Much as we would like to corroborate this observation with a full survey of the rebuffs and diversions suffered by recent visitors to the Eagle Gallery, the brevity of this article – and the 21.30 flight from London City Airport to Hamburg – demands that we limit ourselves to the following two examples.

Art Monthly critic Gregor Heinze arrived at the Eagle Gallery to find a BACK IN 40 MINUTES note pinned to the door. After walking around the block he returned to find that this had been replaced with one that read BACK IN 20 MINUTES. Now, did this mean twenty *additional* minutes to the forty that had already elapsed, or had the proprietor returned to amend the note after deciding that the errand could be completed in half the time? In which case, should the gallery not be open? pondered

Heinze as he went around the block again. The note he found on his return – BACK IN 10 MINUTES – though ostensibly indicating that the moment of entering the gallery was brought nearer with each tour of the block, also suggested a pattern of infinite regression in which the proprietary leave of absence would be halved and halved again – ad infinitum – like a variation on Zeno's Dichotomy Paradox.[1] And so it was: two further tours of the block yielded first a BACK IN 5 (the upbeat nonchalance of which did nothing to mollify the furious critic) and then a BACK SHORTLY. "Shortly?" thought Heinze. "How soon is 'shortly'?"

Breffni Fitzpatrick, unlike all the other visitors to the Eagle Gallery, actually managed to *enter* the building. Inside, he saw:

…An arrow directing me downstairs to the basement. I descended three flights of stairs and found myself in

---

1. I'm a bit pushed for time, but I suppose I should offer a brief summary of this paradox. A man is trying to cover a finite distance. Obviously, in order to reach his goal he must first complete half the total distance. Having completed this half, he must then travel half the remaining distance (i.e., a quarter of the total distance), and then half of *that* half (i.e., an eighth of the total), and then half of each subsequently diminishing distance (locked in the arithmetical series 1/2, 1/4, 1/8, 1/16, 1/32, 1/64…), meaning that he travels an *infinite* number of *finite* distances without ever completing the total distance.[1]

1. I should add that it took me fifteen minutes to recall and write this down – the exact amount of time by which I missed my flight. Although I managed to persuade the check-in staff to put me on the very next plane, I arrived in Hamburg in the early hours of the morning and had to wait half an hour for a cab in freezing fog, so aggravating the virus I had contracted over Christmas that I had to spend the next day in bed, missing the first day of my conference. *Happy now?*[1]

1. And so, having missed the flight, I decided I may as well fritter away a few more minutes by sticking in this miniscule footnote to underpin the theme of infinite regression.

– 150 –

a gloomy vestibule with a door at one end, which I opened. There was a sound piece playing in a pitch-black corridor or passage: here, then, was the art. Groping my way along the wall to the accompaniment of clattering saucepans, crashing cutlery and male voices muttering expletives, I emerged suddenly and to my considerable surprise via a door at the other end of the corridor or passage into the brightly lit kitchen of the neighbouring gastropub, was forced into a chair and aggressively interviewed by the head chef for the vacant post of Chief Dishwasher...

Readers who want to find out how Fitzpatrick fares in his new vocation can find the full article in the February issue of *Parachute*.

Tchüss.

– *Interregnum*, 2005

Coincidence

Coincidence is not something that succumbs to neat rationalization. We tend to think of it only when it happens – say, when bumping into a friend who has booked a holiday at the same obscure vegetarian guest-house in Connemara as we have. "You, here?" we splutter in unison at the breakfast table, each praying that the other has not planned to visit the same heritage centre as we have later that afternoon. In such situations it is better to downplay the coincidence, for once the unlikelihood of our both being *here*, in *this* place, on the *same* day has been remarked on – once this conspiracy between space and time has been duly acknowledged – it dawns on us that we might have to change our itinerary, that we might, in short, have to "do things together". "It would be silly not to," we agree with bashful disingenuousness, knowing full well that this is simply not the case. After all, we have come on holiday to *escape* the familiar, and this includes friends and acquaintances, however misanthropic that may sound.

The alternative is for both parties to behave as though they have never met, to behave as though they are not themselves. Think about it: we are wearing our holiday clothes anyway, and are already thus partly in character.

We have merely to exaggerate this sartorial detour into a psychological one. For if holidays are an escape from the familiar, then surely one's personality should be the first thing to be discarded.

So, when bumping into people we know unexpectedly in Irish guesthouses, we should regard them as generic holidaymakers. We should think of them in the same way that we think of "that nice couple from Croydon", or "Mr Turnbull and his delightful wife, from Sleaford". In other words, the coincidence should be regarded as an opportunity for an armistice, whereby the relationship as it was is dissolved and rebuilt from scratch. Who knows, if the new relationship flourishes, both parties may arrange to meet each other on their return to England. They may even become good friends.

– *European Sociological Review*, 2009

A Soul is a Wheel

When, in April of last year, it became apparent that Sir John Betjeman would soon relinquish the post of Poet Laureate, speculation surrounding his successor naturally began to mount. Some found this speculation distastefully premature, given the graveness of his condition and the certainty that a celebrated life was nearing its end. Even as this national treasure was being carried to his final resting place in St Enodoc churchyard in Cornwall, the media were recalling an event that had happened six years previously: in 1978 Ted Hughes and Philip Larkin had been commissioned to write quatrains commemorating the Silver Jubilee, and in retrospect it is difficult not to see this as a contest between Betjeman's most likely successors.

Although Larkin and Hughes had addressed the theme of nationhood before, when required to explore national identity in direct relation to the monarchy it seemed that both men were found wanting. It is surprising that the embittered Larkin, whose output had dwindled to a clutch of baleful stanzas about drinking and wanking, could find the *inclination* to observe that "In times when nothing stood / but worsened, or grew strange, / there was one constant good: / she did not change." And even more surprising that the prolific Hughes could find the *time* to remark that "A Soul is a Wheel. / A Nation's a Soul / With a Crown at the Hub / To keep it Whole". Though Larkin's is the better poem, neither is particularly distinguished. Hughes's effort is a perfunctory assemblage of innocuous metaphors, written, one feels, with a sceptre held over his cranium. At least Larkin has the guts to use the feminine pronoun, which fosters unexpected and slightly transgressive intimacy, like Michael Fagan wandering into the Queen's bedroom.

Larkin, who also died recently, eventually refused the laureateship, so it fell to an ambivalent Hughes to make as good a fist of it as he could. What was not reported at the time was that, besides the other high-profile candidates hastily lined up as token alternatives to Hughes (and quickly discounted for their republicanism), numerous other writers had expressed interest in the post – though mostly in symbolic protest at the fact that Hughes's appointment should be regarded as such a fait accompli. Of these more obscure, "experimental" authors, Bobby Rimmer was undoubtedly among the more vociferous. Alas, his voice – and it is the voice of darts, a voice of considerable poetic force – was, like so many others, drowned out by the knee-jerk unanimity of the literary cognoscenti, who were so reluctant to extend the debate about the laureateship to the public. Purists asserted that the incumbent should address not just national identity but national identity filtered through the specific lens of the monarchy, while liberals inclined to the view that monarchic content might be sublimated or even eliminated, provided the subject was an edifying one. Now it happened that Rimmer had much to say on the subject of edification, but unfortunately most of it was off-the-record anecdote. There remains only the following poem originally published in the *Daily Mirror* in the days leading up to Hughes's appointment, which I quote here in full:

To Eric Bristow

Never easily impressed by your own work:
the glib brevity of each victory
– a procession of postmen and plumbers
sent back to Ilford or Romford
so *you* could do this for a living,
a smouldering Benson cocked atrociously in one hand
and a nine-dart checkout
pinched like a fountain pen in the other.

A well-drilled indifference my abiding impression,
making a minimum of each maximum,
the Edwardian drape of your hairdo
trembling stiffly in the dull thud of tungsten.
No, never easily impressed by your own work,
like some performers and "creative" types.

Yes, I was also surprised by the verbal restraint shown here by the excitable Geordie. The epic bathos of Rimmer's darts commentary is here exchanged for a simple observation of the facts: Bristow, who has competed in the final of every world championship since 1980 (except 1982, when he suffered a first-round defeat to qualifier Steve Brennan, one of the greatest shocks in darts history), is so good at throwing sharp metal objects at a small target that he doesn't need a day job. But his success means that his opponents must continue *their* day jobs. And his grip on the number-one spot – and by implication the lives of these "postmen and plumbers" – is so effortless and "indifferent" that it can be maintained while chain-smoking: Eric is quite literally *prospering with one hand while killing himself with the other*. Rimmer conveys this with remarkable precision and lightness of touch. Moreover, his description of Bristow's hair – strangely reminiscent of Oscar Wilde's – provides levity in an otherwise deadly serious poem. Without it, the repetition of "never easily impressed by your own work" would seem ponderous.

The last line of the poem has been the subject of much speculation among darts enthusiasts and literary critics alike. For some, "'creative' types" is a reference to those who "create" (a cockney term meaning "make a fuss" or "complain") in protest at Bristow's infamous on-stage gamesmanship and pre-match sledging; while for others it is a pop at those who would belittle darts by comparing it to more "creative" sports.

More generally, it will be noted that the metaphors and similes employed here by Rimmer the poet are, though effective, not quite as vertiginous as those employed by Rimmer the darts commentator. On this subject Rimmer is typically ludic: "Wha' werks oona stage'll nae alwiz werk oona page, man!" Formally, the decision to cast the poem in sonnet form is daring, and ultimately successful, despite the questionable enjambment in the penultimate line of the octet, which is really only *half* a line. To my knowledge this poem is unique. Unique in the sense that it is not only the best poem but the *only* poem the author has published – though as the Voice of Darts he continues to speak poetic*ally* in an astonishingly imagistic repertoire that gives Pound and Williams a run for their money.

But is Eric Bristow a fitting subject for a laureate? Well, we would like you, the reader, to decide. I'm sure you can improve on my cursory appraisal of this poem, and we're offering some very special prizes to those who are willing to try. The best article will win £50 in premium bonds and a ticket to the final of this year's Butlins Masters. The runner-up will receive £25 in premium bonds, and the third-placed submission a £10 book voucher redeemable at WHSmiths and John Menzies. Articles must be 600–800 words in length, not including quotations and footnotes, and must be typed. The best five articles will be published in the July issue of *Wet Feet*.

Hughes was wrong. The Soul might be a Wheel, but at the Hub of this Wheel is not a Crown but a Bull's-Eye, and surmounting this a Treble Twenty and Double Top…

– *Wet Feet*, 1985

Punditry, Television
and the Modern Novel

Did anyone *not* see Silas Whitby's latest novel last night on BBC1? Where on earth were you? Well, you missed a classic. Obviously, unless you've been taking a vacation on another planet you will know the result by now, so the following article should not impair your enjoyment of this evening's extended highlights, which the BBC has put together by popular demand. I myself watched the novel live in a pub in Bermondsey. For those who missed it, here is a summary of the key incidents.

There was a huge cheer as the author, dressed in his trademark dressing gown and filthy jogging bottoms, hair uncombed, breath reeking of coffee, fingers and lips stained by nicotine, emerged from the tunnel and staggered onto the pitch at the Reebok Stadium. Adulation turned momentarily to anxiety as some members of the crowd thought they detected a slight limp in the author's gait. But this turned out to be early-morning stiffness, and fears were quickly dispelled as the Whitbread-nominated novelist went nimbly through his procrastination routine, obsessively rearranging stationery items on his desk and reloading his stapler. The author's colostomy bag was attached, his iMac wheeled out into the centre circle, and the referee, having first checked to ensure the hardware conformed to WA standards and that the assistant referees' and fourth official's stopwatches were synchronized with his own, finally raised the whistle to his lips. He had only to wait for the TV people to confirm that the live feed was in place for the novel to begin.

In the commentary box, John Motson filled these seconds of otherwise dead air time with a diligent, if arcane, statistical profile of the author's previous performances on this ground – which his co-commentator Mark Lawrenson tempered with his usual affectionate wit. Earlier that morning on *Writing Focus*, Lawrenson had drawn attention to the fact that the author had allegedly asked to give a voluntary urine sample before starting the novel, in sarcastic protest at the uncorroborated accusations of stimulant abuse levelled at some of his high-profile peers earlier that week in the tabloid press. This show of solidarity pleased the watching millions and the capacity crowd, who had seen the reputation of the modern novel dragged through the mire these last few weeks. They were also pleased to see that the author, a noted philanthropist and annual participant in Comic Relief, had agreed to wear a red nose for the duration of this particular novel – though overseas viewers were understandably baffled by this.

The novel itself began quietly, with a meandering and somewhat constipated account of a nineteenth-century dowager's grand tour. But then again this was a historical novel, and historical novels are often stylistically unspectacular.

In the twenty-first minute of the novel, just after the author had set the plot in motion and introduced the crowd to the main characters, a middle-aged woman emerged from the dugout shouting something at the dishevelled belletrist. The author ignored the intrusion. The woman repeated herself three times before finally sprinting into the centre circle to confront the author face to face. The on-desk microphones installed to amplify the author's solipsistic mumblings and sighs – and thus enhance our appreciation of the technical nuances of literary composition – broadcast her words to the crowd and the viewing public. She was heard to ask the author whether he wanted a toasted cheese sandwich and a glass of apple juice, and whether, perhaps, he might see his way to picking up the dry-cleaning later on that afternoon. The author waved her away angrily with one hand while continuing to write with the other.

In the thirty-third minute, a balloon drifted onto the pitch. Pursued gamely by its owner, a small girl in a pink dress with her face painted like a tiger's, it was blown directly towards the author, the streamers and string catching around his feet. The author was oblivious as the girl disentangled her balloon from the laces of his dismal moccasins, standing motionlessly for a moment in contemplation of this sedentary monomaniac – whom she no longer recognized as her father – before skipping back to the stand and raising her arms to be lifted over the hoardings by a steward in a visibility vest.

Just a minute later the author's ten-year-old son, clutching a football and wearing a replica Manchester United shirt bearing the name "Paul Scholes", approached the writing desk to ask his father to take him to the park, only to be dismissed even more rudely than the author's wife ten minutes earlier. The small boy was suffered to trudge disconsolately back to his seat in Row G to hoots of derision from a crowd impatient to see how the novel would unfold.

The spectators' admiration of the author's vigilance during these domestic distractions found expression as a series of chants accompanied by Nuremberg Rally-style arm extensions. However, in the forty-third minute their fervour turned to dismay as the author, raising his hand to his chin in a gesture of instinctive contemplation – a gesture he had performed successfully in so many earlier novels – overturned a cup of coffee, tumbling backwards off his chair as he tried to avoid the hot liquid going onto his lap. A physio sprinted onto the pitch to tend to the burns and check that the author had not swallowed his tongue in the fall, but it turned out he had suffered only minor scalding. However, some of the coffee had gone over the keyboard, so the author had to signal to the bench for a replacement. Five minutes of injury time followed at the end of a somewhat fraught first period, and the author was visibly relieved to go in at half-time without sustaining serious narrative injury to his work.

* * *

When the camera cut to the studio analysts, Gary Lineker was surprisingly downbeat. "If you've just joined us," he smiled wryly, "well, frankly you've not missed much... Alan, it's been rather dull hasn't it?" Alan Hansen agreed that the opening and middle part of the novel had been not just dull but "dire, Gary, *dire*". Hansen took us through the first and fourth chapters, replaying the most heinous sequences over and over and commenting, "It juss gets wuss and wuss e'ry taim yer lurk at it." Another pundit whose name no one could recall – probably the manager of a semi-professional novelist drafted in by the BBC to give their coverage more grass-roots appeal – then made several tautological statements about "hard work", "discipline" and "chances", admitting that "the novel, as a novel", had not been a great spectacle. Martin O'Neill went further, stating that it was perhaps the most abysmal novel he had seen all season. Ian Wright saw things differently, praising the novel's diligent plot in typically partisan and emotive fashion, referring to the author by his first name and castigating his fellow pundits' lack of generosity.

As usual, Wright's view was the nation's view. In fact, it was not just the nation's but the *world's* view, for at that moment people as far afield as Gambia and Bhutan were hurling abuse at their TV sets. "These pundits are out of touch, they know nothing of the modern novel," complained plasterer Bob Jenkins as he sat watching the novel in his semi-detached bungalow in Thetford. A waiter in Torquay, a diamond merchant in Holland and a Maltese fisherman were all saying precisely the same thing. As were a team of North Sea oil-riggers, who had downed tools specifically to tune in to the novel on an old black-and-white Samsung with a coat hanger for an aerial. They couldn't understand what the hell Lineker and his team had against this novelist, who in their opinion was the finest since Balzac. "What *more* do they want?" concurred Leonid Khrushchev as he orbited the Earth in the old Soviet space station *Mir*, which had intercepted the BBC transmission on its instruments. The Russian cosmonaut reflected with great sadness that this travesty of opinion would one day give intelligent beings completely the wrong impression of the Blue Planet, as it drifted through deep space into some distant planetary system.

In the second half, the novel gathered pace, unfolding as a historical *roman-à-clef* spanning several centuries, culminating in a remarkable denouement no one had seen coming. Lineker and Co. were required to eat much humble pie in the post-novel analysis, conceding that they had misconstrued the painstaking characterization and topographical description of the novel's first half as a lack of narrative momentum, when in fact the author had been patiently crafting a matrix of interlocking tableaux that would detonate with ingenious timing in a final devastating chapter.

Ian Wright walked out of the studio while the programme was still being broadcast, exuding the dignity of complete punditorial vindication.

– Radio Times, 2010

How We Used to Write

You will appreciate that, as the author of some 900 novels, 200 collections of poetry, 94 volumes of essays and correspondence, 50 biographies, 19 memoirs, 9 travelogues, 5 medical textbooks, 3 unsolicited supplements to *The Joy of Sex* and nearly 1 letter to *You and Yours*, I have spent more time than most people at readings, launches, literary lunches, festivals, conferences and so forth – indeed, I have spent at least as much time at these jamborees as I have behind a closed study door shouting at my wife not to come in. Of the many things asked of authors on the literary circuit, the question "How do you write?" is perhaps the most common. It is intended not just in the sense of how one comes up with the words, but in the sense of how they are physically inscribed onto a surface. My own reply to the question – "With a dagger dipped in hummingbird blood, my dear, with a dagger dipped in hummingbird blood…" – is of course intended to dissuade further enquiry into my actual methods.

It's hard now, in these baroque times, to imagine what writing must have been like for our less fortunate forebears. I refer predominantly, of course, to those authors condemned to live out their literary days in the dreary digital age, when "the daily practice of writing" (to borrow the title of R.B. Hudman's recent account of that era) had reached its nadir – at least in terms of the actual paraphernalia used to "get black on white". We are all familiar, I hope, with the global cataclysm that brought that unhappy epoch to an end. But before considering the literary renaissance engendered by the CHOLESTROL virus, let us briefly recall the period in question.

From 1868, when Christopher Latham Sholes marketed the first practical typewriter, to the early twenty-first century, when the personal computer reigned supreme, we saw a steady decrease in the number of "holographs" (for non-belletrists, that's "manuscripts written in the author's own hand"). But between 2006 and 2016, writers began to rebel against the word processor, and in 2020 the last digitally output document was shredded and interred in a government-controlled landfill site in Corby. As Hudman reminds us in *The Daily Practice of Writing*, this dissatisfaction with the keyboard and screen was, ironically, initially an affectation, "a fad started by internet bloggers who, rather than posting their documents as PDFs, would scan in handwritten fragments to be downloaded as JPEG files". The caprice of these shoe-gazing scriveners was unwittingly prescient. Thanks to the sudden appearance, in 2016, of CHOLESTROL, the global virus that afflicted not just computer terminals but the very cables and wireless bands that connected them (bringing internet traffic to a standstill), word-processed text was rendered virtually useless from a disseminatory viewpoint; for in just a few months the virus became so widespread and pervasive – infesting the cables that linked terminals to their printers, internal CD burners and even the USB ports that enabled the retrieval of data through portable hard and flash drives – that no document written on a computer could be physically extracted from it.

Consumers faced the stark reality that, even if they replaced all their infected hardware with brand-new equipment, they would never be able to link it to any "network" (which word now took on a rather sinister overtone). A significant number, realizing that the recent evolution of personal computers had depended entirely on the notion of connectivity and global information-sharing, opted not to replace it at all – for, suddenly bereft of this vast nexus, bereft now of Hotmail, eBay, MySpace and the like, they had no further use for it. As for the publishing industry in this period, well, the immediate consequences, as Hudman here clarifies, were all too obvious:

> Dissemination became impossible. Where, previously, a text could be sent from Norwich to Nairobi with the click of a mouse, it was now marooned in the geographical place of its creation – at least until writers had replaced their computers and printers with new models. Moreover, because modern typesetting had for a long time been digital, the publishing industry

was thrown into crisis. When the printing technicians replaced their equipment, connected their uninfected brand-new desktop computers to their systems and ran their bitmap software, they wondered why the results were exactly the same as with their infected hardware (i.e. rows of garbled machine code). They eventually realized that the CHOLESTROL virus had lain dormant in the raster image processors of their laser printers, and had, at the instant they hit Print, surged ravenously back into the new computer hardware, colonizing every intermediate electrical node in the system.

Printers were confronted with the prospect of replacing every electrical component of their machinery, while scrapping their brand-new state-of-the-art computer hardware before they had completed even a single job. Needless to say, very little was published that year or the next.

Writers, meanwhile, had simply buried their heads in the sand and carried on writing with such equipment as they had. Most authors had an old electric typewriter in the attic. These Olivettis, Brothers and IBMs were no match for computers, but at least enabled writers to edit and hone their texts on a tiny LCD screen before printing them out, unlike mechanical typewriters, which instantly committed every letter to manuscript form. But whether one used an Olivetti or an ancient Underwood was irrelevant: producing a manuscript was easy; *re*producing it was the problem.

* * *

Suddenly mechanical typesetting was in demand again. Ancient lino- and monotype equipment, long decommissioned and now the property of museums and private collectors, was at a premium. Curators were inundated with requests to loan their machines indefinitely, and were happy to do so at extortionate rates, before finally selling them outright for even more lucrative profit. But where were the people with the skills required to operate these devices? Who, given even a decade with such industrial arcana, might produce such a thing as a novel or an anthology of contemporary verse?

All this may sound somewhat hyperbolic to younger readers, but people of my generation are just about old enough to remember how publishers struggled to adapt this equipment to their needs. The machines, they discovered, were missing vital parts, parts that manufacturers had of course long ceased to produce, so most early neo-mechanical devices were flung together using components from numerous different models. According to Hudman, the first experiments to emerge from the secret factories and abandoned airfields in Norfolk were "tottering behemoths incapable of producing much more than a single dithyrambic convulsion, before breaking down and having to be dismantled".

Thus began a period of difficult readjustment for exponents of the printed word. By now digital typesetters and printers had given up trying to reservice their equipment, and called in the receivers, so the future of publishing lay in the hands of eccentric, determined, but alas untrained syndicates of men who, thanks to the polymathic demands of their project – which had advanced beyond the adaptation of mere printing components to the conscription of *any* object that looked like it might perform the desired function – had little choice but to be part publisher, part typesetter, part engineer, part mechanic, part salvager, part sculptor, part scientist – oh, and not forgetting part *writer*. Yes, writers had finally realized that if their work were ever to see the light of day, they might have to assume a more active role in its physical production than before, and so, from roughly 2023 onwards, tended to be present at any attempt to reproduce it. In fact, the production and *re*production of the work were now a single process, and it became increasingly the case that the writer and his polymathic ensemble worked in a single place at the same time, like a team of contractors.

By now, pessimism had given way to a sort of hysterical romanticism, adopted in no small part, it should be pointed out, in opposition to the ineptitude that charac-terized the Government's handling of the whole affair. The regional tsars appointed to oversee new, state-sanctioned disseminatory methods had succumbed to a common fallacy: the conviction that a text had first to be written and only then to be published. The renegade syndicates, on the other hand, suspected that by abolishing this distinction, by abolishing the manuscript-into-proof convention, the current difficulties could be more easily circumvented. There ensued a new period of authorial collaboration, whereby existing technologies were radically adapted into processes that merged conception, composition, inscription and published document into a single creative act. The "text", which for so long had been something revealed to publisher and printer only at its final stages, now passed through many hands during the course of a typical working day. Hudman's book refers to a number of engravings in the Victoria and Albert Museum depicting some of the more fanciful projects:

We see things as Bruegel might have seen them, from an aerial perspective: assistants, engineers, writers, lexicographers and a small army of general operatives run hither and thither, feeding an indeterminate substance into the hopper of what appears to be a converted sugar-beet harvester. Surmounting this is a Scarab Major, "a waste-management vehicle of late-twentieth-century vintage" (according to the curators' wall text), partially stripped and integrated into the harvester with an exoskeleton of hydraulic mechanisms. And surmounting *this* is the writer, housed in a cockpit-cum-conning-tower, a control panel of levers and buttons across his lap and chest, wires extending therefrom into a helmet covering the occipital region of the head, imperious yet unsteady on this wedding cake of technology, like a Victorian botanist borne haplessly through the jungle on an elephant.

On closer inspection, it becomes apparent that the indeterminate substance is not being fed *into* but is issuing *from* the machine – which is actually harvesting beet. The "writing" process, then, is evidently a by-product of normal agricultural activity. We can establish this because the writer is not – as we would expect of a writer – looking down at his "desk", then looking up occasionally into middle distance and reading his words back to himself in a state of borderline psychosis; rather, his gaze is fixed on the furrows of discarded vegetation that the machine leaves in its wake. These, we can just about discern, do not conform to the expected linear arrangement, but deviate eccentrically from right to left in a contrived yet random pattern reminiscent of the teeth on a hurdy-gurdy drum. Finally, in the distance is a helicopter. A neighbouring engraving depicts the scene inside. A man in a harness leans over an opening in the belly of the chopper, sending navigational instructions to the pilot on his headset. The caption, "*A scanner about his business*", indicates that it is his job to photograph each field in its topographical entirety…

The reader is now anticipating the description of a third engraving depicting the conversion of this "topographical" information into legible text. Alas, it is not forthcoming. For not a single novel, essay or poem of this period advanced any closer to actual mass reproduction and distribution than at the outset of the CHOLESTROL virus. As can be gleaned from

Hudman's vivid description, much wonderful kinetic sculpture was produced, but no book. Appeals were made to authors known for their eccentric approaches to composition. Unfortunately William Burroughs was long dead, and a medium's attempt to contact Tristan Tzara was unsuccessful. Phone calls were made to a ninety-five-year-old J.G. Ballard, who professed cold delight at the jeopardy of the printed word and by implication literature, unmoved by sycophantic references to the "steam-powered computer" mentioned in his own introduction to his *Complete Short Stories*, and by all similar appeals to his intellectual vanity. And so developments continued without informed consultation, all too often recalling the slapstick melancholia of a Victorian flying machine launched off the end of a pier.

Most readers will be familiar with the first pioneering texts that eventually emerged from this crucible of outlandish experimentation. But to explain how we got from the above impasse to the copious amount of publications we enjoy today requires a more focused account of literature's darkest hour.

With the exception of Howard Jacobson's *Purple Pongistes* (an anthology of Rabelaisian table-tennis literature), most of the first texts produced in the post-digital age were reworkings of the classics. The reason for this was not literary but logistical. As Hudman points out, the machinery required to (re)produce the text "was invariably unreliable, often chewing the author's words into a bolus of incomprehensible characters, forcing them to begin again from scratch". After a succession of spectacular failures, it became standard practice to test the reproductive capacity of machinery using *existing* prose, which could simply be fed into it by assistants. Here is Hudman's account of the evolution of a well-known classic, one of the first to be produced using such methods:

J.K. Rowling's version of *Finnegans Wake* has been a staple of the national syllabus for twenty years now, but how many schoolchildren know that it began life as a mere "test book" for the Hussey Ferguson Press? Literary historians have tended to downplay the role of Hussey Ferguson in the post-CHOLESTROL publishing era, but their first imprint arguably merits placement alongside the *Diamond Sutra* or Caxton's *Recuyell of the Histories of Troy*, for it set the pattern for the early hydrocarbon systems adopted by subsequent disseminators. Previously a manufacturer of plant machinery for the petrochemical industry, Hussey Ferguson's unexpected but historic move into publishing came on 21st August 2025 as a result of a phone call from Rowling's despairing project manager [the contemporary equivalent of an "agent"]. Rowling's team of scientists, engineers, lexicographers, welders, mechanics and psychologists had laboured for three years to convert an oil refinery in Hull to her literary requirements. The wiring and transitional phasework were complex and by no means satisfactorily road-tested, but Rowling's task force – doubtless motivated by promises of substantial bonuses for delivering the book ahead of schedule – had nonetheless seen fit to press their equipment into operation before performing all the necessary diagnostic checks. The results were catastrophic. The explosion in the central reactor sent smoke billowing into the atmosphere. The only thing salvaged from the blast – which was heard as far away as Sleaford and Peterborough – was John Lanchester's witty Foreword.

Enter Michael Chase, Hussey Ferguson's research guru and industry troubleshooter. Just a week after being dispatched to Rowling's writing plant, Chase had steered the project to its completion. How did he turn things around? The bookish Chase, a Bachelor of Science and former *Mastermind* finalist, had lugged a paperback edition of *Finnegans Wake* everywhere he had been for about a decade, without ever having really engaged, if he was honest with himself, with the text's manifold literary subtleties. In fact, it had lain untouched on the dashboard of his car for three years, fading in the sun like an old road atlas. "Why not finally put it to good use?" he thought to himself.

The impact of this modernist classic was immediate. Where Rowling's prose had left non-condensable deposits on the pipes connecting the vacuum distillator to the feed hydrotreater (resulting in a build-up of pressure in the atmospheric distillation tanks), Joyce's oneiric stream of consciousness was a laxative

to the whole process. Rowling had merely to oversee operations from a hydraulic chair high above
the blending pool, where she fashioned the freshly
hydrocracked and isomerized orthographic symbols
into a phantasmagoric blockbuster pumped directly
into the nation's homes.

The 2032 publication of this novel was a catalyst for
cultural change – not least because the mortality rate
among workers on Rowling's project was the lowest
seen in the publishing industry in a decade.

There soon followed a number of works that need no
introduction, for they now stand as a seminal canon.
With the exception of the earlier mentioned work by
Jacobson, all these texts were published in non-book
form. Let us deviate momentarily from our technical
concerns to consider their *literary* impact.

Julie Burchill's revisitation of T.S. Eliot's *The Waste
Land* was broadcast continuously through tannoys at
shopping centres throughout south-east England from
2033–38. Eliot's famous sequence was supplemented
by a prologue and epilogue of Burchill's own devising.
The function of the prologue is to delegate each of the
five cantos to a different narrator. Vivid contextual and
psychogeographical detail is supplied here so that we
are left in no doubt that this chorus of lost souls is to be
taken as the modern equivalent of a gang of "chavs".
Moreover, the sequence – translated into "chavic" line for
line – is accompanied by stage actions and establishing

captions which, had the piece been written in text form, would've been rendered in italics. Instead, they are spoken by policemen (as if reading from their notebooks in a magistrate's court), placing us firmly in the cultural landscape of early-twenty-first-century *Ingerlund*, a "wasteland" of globalized consumerism, pub-carpark fights and adolescent shootings carried out in the meaty waft of KFC extraction vents. Finally, Burchill introduces us to Big Chief Sittingbourne, the "half Injun, half chav" visionary whose job it is to draw moral lessons from the sayings of his "redoubtable braves" in a pithy but disaffected epilogue set to R&B. It is a powerful piece of work, in which Kent is seen to assume the redemptive mantle of physically incarnating the *meta*physical wasteland evoked in Eliot's original poem.

George Courtney's novel *The Ascent of Righteous Beasts: How Much Longer Will I Be Able to Inhabit the Divine Sepulchre of Oddbins, Waitrose, etc.* began as a rumour started by the author in a pub in Chingford in December of 2032, and quickly spread to neighbouring counties, where it gained narrative embellishment with every retelling. However, when this word-of-mouth piece finally got back to the author (who had not moved from his bar stool in the intervening years), he disowned it, complaining that readers had perverted his original intentions. Nevertheless, the "text" remains at large, like the urban myth some claim it was always intended to be.

Another breakthrough work was Arthur Seagrove's *Reed All about Me*, which, though originating from an existing book, also eschewed typographical transcription, consisting as it did of the author simply reliving the life of the actor Oliver Reed, as chronicled in the latter's 1979 autobiography of the same title. Originally planned as a novel, this work was soon revised as a novella and eventually cut down to a somewhat inconclusive short story as the alcohol wreaked havoc on the author's health. Few could keep pace with Oliver Reed, and Seagrove's work was understandably criticized for its lack of fidelity to the original text. On page 103 of Reed's book we find the following passage:

"I wonder if my aunt keeps any brandy about the place," I said craftily as we staggered indoors, knowing that she didn't but with my mind fixed firmly on his Vat 69.

"I don't think so," said the Colonel, "but I've got some whisky."

"Oh, have you really?" I said. And we went into his room and polished off the Vat 69, then started on the Gordon's and polished that off too. He looked sorrowfully at the empty bottles and I said never mind, St Patrick's Day was only once a year. He said he was glad as we had just drunk his whole month's supply of liquor.

By contrast, Day 103 – the final day – of Seagrove's version finds the author vomiting blood in a private clinic in Bedfordshire. Nothing has been heard of him since.

* * *

However much of a curate's egg Seagrove's work may
have been, many saw fit to follow its performative example. I gladly count myself among their number, for
it remains a pivotal text, linking literary epochs of remarkable – some have said unbridgeable – dissimilarity.
Its publication augmented the belief that literature
should no longer consist of permanent documents fro-
zen for ever in time as "books". Authors realized that
the abolition of the distinction between manuscript and
proof engendered by the CHOLESTROL virus had
merely been a prelude to an even greater dissolution: of
the boundary between language and reality, the event
and its representation (in whatever form). Not only was
there now no "proof" of an original "text" to be constantly
amended up to the final hour of publication, there was no
distinction between the *time* of the text's writing and that
of its publication. Publication was no longer something
put on record for ever, a book on a library shelf, say,
but an evanescent phenomenon in the here and now of
instant public appraisal. The experience of "reading" was
no longer one of linear progression but one of sensorial
immersion in the present.

The New Novels – many of which were written by
me and my peers – were not representational vehicles
but events that unfolded in ostensible reality; not "plays"
(they had no script) but texts offering tangible phenomena in place of typographic symbols or verbal utterances. The referents to which such symbols and utterances

might have formerly referred were now employed as a primary text in its own right – as though Derrida's famous claim that there is "no outside of the text" (i.e. no real separation between the things referred to by a text and the language used to make those references) had been pursued to its logical conclusion. "Why offer a typographically rendered text to be outside *of*?" we asked ourselves.

Readers of our work, or "superintended reality" as we liked to call it, were admittedly few and far between to begin with – chiefly because it became very difficult to distinguish between "authored" reality and plain reality: people didn't know when they were "reading" and when they were merely absorbing sensory data in the usual fashion. To this end, some authors, I regret to say, saw fit to employ "signers" to stand before the various authored spectacles and commentate on them in a language not unlike that used to translate speech for the deaf, thus enabling the populace to distinguish this new literature from surrounding events. It's difficult to convey to the contemporary reader the extent of this ontological confusion between the phenomenology of the text and that of the substrate reality, but picture, if you can, a world in which every other scenario is accompanied by a person standing to one side of it furiously making complicated hand gestures, like those people superimposed onto the Sunday omnibus editions of *Hollyoaks* that you may remember watching as children in the early part of this century. Luckily, these signers were only an interim measure adopted to "break" this new literature to a middlebrow audience.

"Surely 'literature' of this kind," I can hear the reader complaining, "is being written all the time by every living human being." But we must distinguish here between authors and writers. We are all writers, but only some of us are authors. You see, there is the issue of *commentary*. In the essay 'Why I Write', George Orwell traces his literary compulsion to early-childhood thought processes. For instance, he might be sitting on a bench, or moving from the kitchen to the dining room in his house. He writes initially of the kind of background commentary that almost everyone supplies to their daily routine: "I am sitting on a bench… I am moving from the kitchen to the dining room." It's a short step, he contends, from such banal solipsism to something approaching literary representation. Compare the aforementioned commentary to "Young Master George collapsed on a nearby bench, exhausted after his adventures", or "Orwell, roused from his drunken slumber by the clatter of the letterbox, somehow prised his body off the kitchen table and dragged it through to the parlour, catching his head on the gas meter, meaning that he was filled with even greater injustice and self-loathing than usual on opening his mail to find no fewer than three rejection slips for his recent novel *1984*. It was January." We can disregard the author's self-pitying back story here, his clumsy intimations of writerly delinquency and his pathetic attempt to supply calendrical pathos. Ignore all this, and just note the change in tense and the substitution of the first for the third person. And there, in a nutshell, you have it: literary representation. Literary representation is nothing more than the acceptance that a given event, plausible or implausible, real or imagined, can be described and commentated on from different temporal perspectives and by people other than the immediate protagonists.

All the rest is window dressing. So throw your *Collins Dictionary of Literary Terms* on the fire, my child, and follow me into the light. With us authors, you see, the "lived" reality and the commentary on it occur simultaneously. In fact, more often than not, the commentary *precedes* the lived reality. Yes, it's perfectly true: the author may awake with the words "Ashton guided the shuttle through the planet's blazing ionosphere to rescue the doomed colonists…" going around in his head, and sure enough, later on that day, he will find himself orbiting a planet in some distant galaxy.

You now understand why the works listed at the beginning of this treatise are so great in number. My corpus is indeed an extensive one. For I have lived all that I have written, and written all that I have lived. Except that letter to *You and Yours*, which is bothering me, and which I am thinking of rewriting as a cross-channel swim.

– *Interregnum*, 2064

Terminal Velocity

We are falling, falling, falling... This we know: we must hit the ground soon, or at some point in the future, no matter how distant, for it stands to reason that our descent is, surely, the result of the gravitational pull of a body somewhere below. But none ever make it: we are born, live and die in a state of perpetual falling. We live in fear of imminent impact, but our lives are never curtailed by *actual* impact: we simply die of natural causes – and continue falling.

Sight, hearing, smell, taste: we do not know whether we *lack* these faculties or whether there is nothing *to* see, hear, smell or taste. Touch? Feel? The turbulence imparted by terminal velocity certainly induces a horripilation of what we *suppose* is flesh, though whether this can be called "feeling" is debatable. The motion of a deadweight through space is the only confirmation of our existence; the size and nature of our bodies and the magnitude of the space through which they plummet have never been established, for complete paralysis precludes autonomous movement, preventing verification of our corporeal extent. The fact that we cannot shake a limb (if limbs we have) and thereby ascertain where our bodies end means that we cannot rule out the possibility that they *have* no end, that they extend infinitely in all directions; that our corporeality, rather than punctuating space, usurps it entirely.[1] In the eyes of some, then, we do not "fall", for there is no space through which to plummet: the "horripilation" is produced not by terminal velocity but by the molecular oscillation of a single univocal body. And of course there is nothing "below" exacting gravitational influence, for there *is* no below, no above, no yonder. All is within. There is no without, only an illimitable corporeal homogeneity that subsumes "you", "me" and everyone else under a single cosmic solipsism.

Some sages have answered – though with more than a hint of sarcastic dialecticism – that "…our bodies, far from usurping all space, extend no further than a single atom, that 'humanity' is a hailstorm of tiny monads raining down through fathomless oblivion, each with its own minute quota of individuality, a monsoon of putative plumbers, electricians, butchers, barristers, insurance salesmen, quantity surveyors, warehouse operatives, architects, builders, painters, psychiatrists, farmers, historians, loss adjustors, prostitutes, snooker referees, cardiologists, global-equities strategists, lecturers, textile designers, sailors, athletes, obstetric anaesthetists, secretaries, locksmiths, blacksmiths, policemen, tinkers, TV evangelists, cycle couriers, hoteliers, soldiers,

---

1. I should qualify the word "entirely" by adding that advocates of the solidity theory have posited, within the atrocious filaments of this infinitely extending corporeality, the existence of spherical spatial pockets, "planetary negatives" that, structurally, are to the universe what the arch is to the bridge or viaduct.

waste-management consultants, librarians, carpenters, cosmonauts, writers, pornographers, pensioners, dramatists, shepherds, crooks, priests, civil servants, chauffeurs, dinner ladies, movie directors, biologists, cosmologists, monks, gardeners, tramps – men and women with a sense of what they *would* do given more ontologically favourable circumstances: beings in whom there inhered, against all expectation, an unshakeable vocational conviction."

– *The Amateur Cosmographer*, 1993

Mike Harte – Make Art

The following was written to accompany the opening of Jamie Shovlin's installation *Mike Harte – Make Art* at Ashwin Street Gallery, 10th November 2006.

Mike Harte is a friend with whom I studied during my undergraduate degree in fine art. He was renowned for his struggle to make anything that could be labelled "work". What is more, unbeknown to him yet clearly apparent to his fellow students, Mike himself, as well as his struggle, became both the content and product of his output.

During the two years of my postgraduate study, Mike kept in contact. He regularly sent me envelopes filled with newspaper and magazine clippings and other general miscellany that Mike thought would interest me. In total, Mike sent thirty-six envelopes, each of which is featured in its entirety over the pages of the scrapbook Mike Harte – Make Art.

I hope that the upshot of this one-way correspondence was, if nothing else, the development of a pretext for Mike Harte to make art. Of course, he had no idea of this at the time of sending each of these envelopes.

– Jamie Shovlin, introduction to the scrapbook
Mike Harte – Make Art

As an activity with no obvious formal context to define its outcomes, Mike Harte's one-way correspondence with Jamie Shovlin seems not so much a consciously artistic practice as an example of creativity playing truant from art – though Jamie's doormat and the postal routes through which Mike's flamboyant envelopes went their merry way can be considered a context of sorts. The notion of the artwork as something engendered by and representing a relationship between two or more correspondents is of course nothing new, but to lend the informality of private correspondence the stark formality and publicity of gallery/book presentation is surely to risk antagonizing that relationship. Unless I have misread him, Jamie's presentational motives seem poised between generosity and curiosity: the altruism of temporarily suspending one's own concerns and taking the time to showcase a friend's worldview is offset by a pensive anticipation as to what, exactly, the world will make of that view.

Despite an evident fascination with the material that comprises this project, Jamie's stewardship of it is characterized by impartiality and authorial invisibility. Sure, he attaches his name to it, but as facilitator rather than "appropriator": unlike with some of his earlier work (at the ICA and Tate Britain), our appraisal of the gathered material is filtered through no specific epistemological context – other than the cultural radar of a citizen named Mike Harte. And, yes, the author of this text, having seen Jamie's *Lustfaust*[1] at the ICA, *has*

---

1. *Lustfaust: A Folk Anthology 1976–81* is a 2004 work comprising "memorabilia" relating to a fictional German krautrock band.

countenanced the possibility that this person may be an apocryphal creation, despite the convincing biographical back story supplied one evening in some wretched *faux*-Mexican pub on Balls Pond Road. It doesn't really matter to me either way: it happens that Jamie's caught me at a particularly "factitious" moment, and I can think of nothing better than to be willingly enticed into a vindication of an imaginary artist. However, such generosity comes with a considerable rider: I get the chance to write about a friend from *my* past.

The title *Mike Harte – Make Art* sounds less like a description of, or judgement on, something that has already been produced than an exhortation *to* produce. Usually, it is the past that is invoked to evaluate an exhibition's success; as viewers, we make a number of critical judgements that boil down to a single question: What difference does it make? Although the many newspaper clippings that constitute the bulk of Mike's correspondence can be said to document a recent past (that of a nation and that of a citizen of that nation), it is the *future* that hangs over this project, in that our critical judgements boil down to a slightly different question: What difference *will* it make... to Mike? The implication is that the real reason for collating this material into an installation and book has not yet come to pass: as Jamie says, it is "the development of a pretext... to make art". Even if it achieves nothing else, *Mike Harte – Make Art* emphasizes something we usually overlook: that exhibitions have a tense. Thanks to the ubiquitous and specious use of the word "contemporary" in visual art, that tense is often assumed to be the present. Well, it's not the case here.

To dwell further on the specific relationship that exists between Jamie and Mike would be unwise, for I've never met Mike and I've only met Jamie once. Of greater interest to me are the comparisons I began to make between Mike and certain of my own friends as Jamie described the events that led to the production of this book and show. When he first told me about the material acquired through his long correspondence with Mike Harte – and of his decision to become its artistic executor – I was reminded of people from my own past: people who, despite a prolific creative output, for one reason or another did not care, or did not know how, to disseminate their "work" in a formal sense. I thought specifically of one Brendan Fahy, with whom I lived for five years while studying foundation and undergraduate fine art, and who, in retrospect, it seems to me, developed a similarly truant creativity to that of Mike Harte. I hope Jamie and Mike will not think it too indulgent if I mention him here at some length. I do so partly by way of purging guilt that I did nothing to encourage this unpolished genius of piss-your-pants-funny drawings, one-liners, captions, clippings, epigrams, poems, plays, collages, conceptual stunts and impromptu "enunciations" on to greater things, and partly because this is probably the only opportunity I shall get to set down some of his exploits on paper.

* * *

I'm sure we all have at least one friend who deserves to have an essay written about them, someone whose worldview is at fascinating variance with one's own. In my experience, such friends are not so much men and women as poems that have assumed human form. I've no idea whether Mike Harte is such a person to Jamie Shovlin, but Brendan Fahy certainly was to me. To borrow a phrase from Poe, Brendan was an "imp of the perverse", his creative impetus being a curiosity as to what would unfold if the most ill-advised course of action were taken. His output straddled the two years we spent together on a foundation course and the three years I spent as an undergraduate in Nottingham – where, despite an unsuccessful application to the same course, Brendan came to live with me. Brendan was an astonishing draughtsman, but had no interest in capitalizing on his ability. At the beginning of our foundation course, he would always finish his five-hour life study in an hour, and spend the rest of the afternoon defacing his work with sundry transgressions – snake tongues, swastikas, cocks – that were even more impeccably executed than the initial study. While, in themselves, these were probably his least interesting creations, it was nevertheless amusing to watch someone ruin his own work as his peers struggled to emulate it. It's not as if Brendan did this every week, but he did it often enough to throw into question how, exactly, "talent" is to be deployed – and in a context in which the display of talent was regarded as the sole criterion of artistic value.

In fact, it was not through visual work but through text that Brendan made his first real breakthrough. In a constipated art history essay on Romanticism, he inserted, between two sentences, the word "Fuck" – specifically, one feels, to test whether or not it would actually be read. It was. Had he written his essay on a word processor, this indiscretion might conceivably have been construed as a cataclysmic, trans-document typo, but the fact that it was handwritten left no room for such lenient interpretation: this was intentional provocation, unprecedented in more than a decade of the BTEC National Diploma at Norfolk Institute of Art & Design. The art-history tutor took it badly, and Brendan was hauled before Rod Newlands, Senior Lecturer in Foundation Studies, who administered the mildest of rebukes through barely contained laughter. (Much later, the same lecturer, on proofreading Brendan's undergraduate application form and noticing that under the section "Ambitions" he had written "gypsy", could not contain that laughter.)

Brendan's subsequent experiments with text bore the more recognizable stamp of experimental literature, encompassing poetry, drama and the epigram. Of this work, his verse – written in an aphoristic-lyrical style reminiscent of the Ostrobothnian poet Gösta Ågren – was considered his most accomplished. This was his most memorable poem:

The Delightful Sunset

Sun getting lower in the sky.

*

Delightful.

– 196 –

The separation of the first and second lines not merely into stanzas but into *cantos* is particularly audacious – though I hope my transcription of these words from memory (rather than from the original manuscript, long since lost) has not imparted an inadvertent "literariness".

As to Brendan's visual work, the combination of drawing, collage and text that first appeared in the winter of 1989–90 bore no resemblance to anything produced by day under tutorial guidance. Diligent student that I was, I spent the evenings at an easel in my attic room, painting dowdy interiors and pious portraits of my friends, during which endeavours I would sometimes have occasion to reproach Brendan for not following my example and making good use of his prodigious natural ability. One evening, by way of goading Brendan into action, I somewhat foolhardily challenged him to a drawing competition: I proposed that we each repair to a different room in the house and attempt to draw its entire contents in an hour, a challenge he accepted with uncharacteristic zeal. Later, returning from the kitchen with copious charcoal studies of cutlery, appliances and foodstuffs, I asked to see Brendan's work. He handed me a sheet of foolscap paper. On it was a biro sketch of two expressionless characters standing in a park, accompanied by a caption that read: "Dave and his father play ball in the park. Dave has cancer."

Brendan's more "conceptual" pieces, though gauche at first (for a 1991 college project he "went topical", submitting a pound of lard bearing the inscription "Death to Saddam, kill him now before he spreads his evil seed"), soon established a more sophisticated rubric, culminating in a 1996 piece for which he cut a picture of the business tycoon Tiny Rowland out of the newspaper, framed it, placed it on the mantelpiece, and pretended to his flatmates, for an entire year, that it was his father. Another piece was made in response to a dismal guesthouse in which he and I had stayed on moving to Great Yarmouth to pursue our studies. Our relationship with the landlady, Mrs Wickman, was fraught from the outset. After a week we had soiled our room with oil paint and tobacco, played music too loudly, woken our host's elderly mother by coming home in the small hours, and cast doubt on the edibility of her cooking. These latter aspersions, usually mumbled *sotto voce* after her husband – who served as waiter – had deposited our dinner on the table and gone back into the kitchen, were one day offered far too audibly. An argument ensued, and we were forced to voice the unanimous opinion that Mrs Wickman's food was not up to much. At which point Mrs Wickman stormed out of the kitchen and let us have it, giving us notice there and then. Anyway, Brendan's response was to pin a poster on the student notice board advertising an ORIENTAL BAZAAR at 16 Gorleston Road – Mrs Wickman's house. We did not bother to verify whether anyone turned up to the bazaar; the appeal of the work was strictly metaphysical.

* * *

Why did I allow Brendan to think that such acts were mere frippery, when I knew full well that they had more to do with art than anything I'd seen at the institution where I was studying? Perhaps because I was unsure about how things done solely to amuse friends would withstand public scrutiny, especially given the quotidian context of their execution. Nevertheless, a few years later I discovered David Shrigley's work and thought of what might have been, had Brendan been a little better informed and a little less suspicious of the "art world" – at which he looked genuinely askance.

But "informed" was not in Brendan's vocabulary. And this, by way of dragging things back to the matter at hand, appears to be where he and Mike Harte would differ. Where Brendan's deeds were essentially the impromptu actions of a cultural sceptic, Mike's collation of tabloid news clippings into a rolling portrait of the national psyche engages discursively with culture – however unedifying and venal that culture may be. In answer to the question of what difference this public display of his correspondence might make to Mike Harte, surely Arts Council funding will be found to employ him on a permanent basis as Curator of Salient Trivia. Those who hardly ever read the red tops *need* people like Mike to tell them that a piece of masonry once fell on Vanessa Feltz while "she was trying to remove the line 'Vanessa Feltz has a big hairy merkin' from a message wall at a Big Breakfast farewell bash". Somehow, the news that "Rugby star Paul Grayson's wife is to have twins early by Caesarean so the Northampton Saints player can be at Saturday's Powergen Cup Final" – well, somehow, that news *is* important, for believe or not, it had never occurred to me that childbirth, under certain contingencies, could be viewed as a movable feast. Oh, and I'm genuinely grateful to Mike for taking the time to cut out of the *Daily Star* a short piece on "TEN CELEBRITIES WHO ARE PART RED INDIAN".

I should also like to apologize to him for implying earlier that he might not exist.

Long Division

Seventeen thousand eight hundred and sixty-nine, divided by sixty-two.

No problem: sixty-twos into one hundred and seventy-eight goes two (2), leaving fifty-four. Sixty-twos into fifty-four won't go, so bring the six down to make five hundred and forty-six. Sixty-twos into five hundred and forty-six goes eight (8), leaving fifty. Sixty-twos into fifty won't go, so bring the nine down to make five hundred and nine. Sixty-twos into five hundred and nine goes eight (8), leaving thirteen. Sixty-twos into thirteen won't go, so bring down the decimal nought to make one hundred and thirty. Sixty-twos into one hundred and thirty goes two (2), leaving six. Sixty-twos into six won't go, so borrow the second decimal nought to make sixty. Sixty-twos into sixty won't go either (0), so borrow the third decimal nought to make six hundred. Sixty-two into six hundred goes nine (9), leaving forty-two. Sixty-twos into forty-two won't go, so borrow the fourth decimal nought to make four hundred and twenty. Sixty-twos into four hundred and twenty goes six (6), leaving forty-eight. Sixty-twos into forty-eight won't go, so borrow the fifth decimal nought to make four hundred and eighty. Sixty-twos into four hundred and eighty goes seven (7), leaving forty-six. Sixty-two into forty-six won't go, so borrow the sixth decimal nought to make four hundred and sixty. Sixty-twos into four hundred and sixty goes seven (7), leaving twenty-six. Sixty-twos into twenty-six won't go, so borrow the seventh decimal nought to make two hundred and sixty. Sixty-twos into two hundred and sixty goes four (4), leaving twelve. Sixty-twos into twelve won't go, so borrow the eighth decimal nought to make one hundred and twenty. Sixty-twos into one hundred and twenty goes once (1), leaving fifty-eight. Sixty-twos into fifty-eight won't go, so borrow the ninth decimal nought to make five hundred and eighty. Sixty-twos into five hundred and eighty goes nine (9), leaving twenty-two. Sixty-two into twenty-two won't go, so borrow a tenth decimal nought to make two hundred and twenty. Sixty-twos into two hundred and twenty goes three (3).

At this point you have the number 288.2096774193. That's how many times sixty-two will go into seventeen thousand, eight hundred and sixty-nine. Except that we're not through yet, for there's still the issue of the remaining thirty-four left over from when we just did sixty-twos into two hundred and twenty, just now. But you need a piss, you're *dying* for a piss. That's OK, go for one. In fact, why not fix yourself a sandwich, check your email, make some calls, generally put your life in order? And then return to your desk rejuvenated, resisting the temptation to round the last decimal place of the figure in front of you – the figure 288.2096774193 – up or down. Instead, simply take your pencil and bring that *eleventh* decimal nought down to make the thirty-four into three hundred and forty, which, divided by sixty-two, gives five (5), leaving thirty. Now, sixty-twos will no more go into thirty than a rich man will enter the kingdom of heaven, so you're going to have to borrow a twelfth decimal nought to make three hundred. But don't worry, my use of the word "borrow" has been figurative all along; there's an unlimited supply of these decimal noughts and no one is going to ask you to pay any of them back.

Continuing then: sixty-twos into three hundred goes four (4), leaving fifty-two, which, being a smaller number than sixty-two, forces us to take yet another nought, the thirteenth in total, make five hundred and twenty, and divide *that* by our old friend sixty-two, the veteran of some sixteen consecutive calculations, who is just about dead on his feet and longing for that magic moment when the remainder of the next calculation is *an exact multiple of himself*, say, one hundred and twenty-four, one hundred and eighty-six or two hundred and forty-eight. Oh sweet Jesus, what he wouldn't give for such a number. Will it *ever* happen? There are probably Harvard mathematicians who could glance at this long division, see a pattern and give him a straight yes or no. He could sure use a short cut like that – I don't know, some kind of algorithm or something. It's not like he doesn't have other things to do. Tomorrow, for instance, he is being multiplied by the square root of $(6x - 4y)^3$ by a lecturer at De Montfort who's been commissioned to look into the maths behind ternary superconductors. Obviously, sixty-two needs to be at the top of his game for this calculation.

So, if anyone knows how he can get the hell out of this long division, please speak up.

— Brontosaurus, 1981

Six Applications for Friendship

Part I

I have been asked by the editors of *The European Sociological Review* to say a few words on the theme of "The Milieu". I was once at the centre of a rather exciting milieu. Indeed, it is no exaggeration to say that I was the hub of a social wheel that spun very quickly – and spanned more salons than I care to mention. This, I suppose, is the story of how I dismantled it. I say "story"; it is really nothing more than a prosaic description of my preferred method for obtaining friends.

I received twenty-three applications for friendship this year – three down on last year, but never mind. Anyway, I soon whittled these down to a shortlist of six. Three of these applicants had approached me personally, which is not something I usually encourage. Of the other three, one had been invited to upgrade from "correspondent", another had applied for full friendship, despite already having been told there was no possibility of advancing beyond the level of "acquaintance" (a decision I have since reviewed in light of the reduced applications – I commend the applicant for his persistence), while the third was an undergraduate who had shown ample credentials on an orienteering weekend I attended in the New Forest, and whose application I solicited anonymously by leaving my card on his bunk bed.

Before reviewing these six applications for friendships, I will describe why and how I came to formalize the process of *gaining* friends. Having outlined my rubric thus and given a short history of its development, I will then go on to consider the merits of the shortlisted applicants in Part II of this essay, to be published in the spring issue of this journal. The reader should prepare itself for a certain amount of technical jargon, for a comprehensive description of the process will entail quoting occasionally from the prospectus sent out to potential candidates.

The escalating vocational and domestic demands of adulthood jeopardize what the child in us insists on calling our "individuality", and in our attempts to "find space for ourselves" we often neglect our friendships. Even the most established can dwindle to a charade of hollow salutations and dutiful stop-and-chats – a moribund catechism sustained more by habit than mutual enthusiasm. *It happens*: friends once integral to one's life now accessorize it. But then again friendships cannot, like saplings planted in urban streets by well-meaning local authorities, be allowed to grow unchecked into gargantuan Yggdrasils. If they are to coexist they must be pruned, pollarded – *coppiced* if need be. Mortgages, careers and a family are the natural methods; it was my misfortune to arrive at a more particular husbandry only after my friends had deserted me. But before proffering your sympathy, consider that it was the combustion of these friendships that set me on my present course; know that I owe my current methodology entirely to the short shrift of those to whom I was once closest. Ah, *closeness*, *intimacy* – I have not uttered these words for a decade, and I find they leave a nostalgic taste in my mouth. The sad reality of friendships is that, far from advancing on to levels of ever increasing intimacy, most reach a ceiling of intimacy beyond which it is impossible to advance. The friendship's future comes to depend on its perpetual levitation at this level – or else it fades and the ceiling of intimacy becomes, in retrospect, the apogee of a trajectory.

My system of formal application renounces this paradigm of subjective intimacy for one of distance and objectivity. It has not been as difficult to implement as you might imagine, for my friends were beginning to have less room for me in their diaries – my "life plan" having diverged greatly from their own without either of us ever acknowledging the fact. From their careerist viewpoints I must have appeared like a hamstrung sprinter in a race: going backwards as they were just hitting their stride. Success and prosperity had conquered their every waking hour, while my failure to share their vocational, material and domestic obsessions meant that my own diary was a tabula rasa. So I decided to act. My initial experiments were not, as my friends thought, perverse exit strategies from my milieu, but straightforward diagnostic inspections of the prevailing social status quo.

Most of these experiments took the form of gatherings held at my house. I once gave a party at which each guest had been told to arrive at a different time. The idea was inspired by frustration with party guests who, despite my horary specifications, tended to show up whenever they liked. Let us admit that, whether the time of a guest's arrival is contrived or not, it *conveys* something to the host – who is more sensitive than is commonly realized to the first arrivals' tremors of mortification and the Warholian aloofness of latecomers. Now, one *can* manipulate the arrival of one's guests – to a degree. For example, if you want them to come at eight you tell them to come at seven. This is standard practice. But whatever you do there is always, it seems, an hour between the first and last arrivals. The latter assume, or pretend to assume – and this is a generous analysis, I know – that the host will require this extra hour for last-minute preparations. To me this is an insult. Cometh the hour, am I to be found manically crashing pots and pans, slamming cutlery drawers and scraping burnt victuals from the ceiling? No, I am to be found standing by the mantelpiece in freshly pressed evening wear, fiddling with my watch chain, the food laid out before me on the sideboard, the mayonnaise turning translucent in the encroaching dusk…

It was on just such an occasion, in just such a position, that I first wondered whether my guests' "staggered" arrivals could be used as the basis for a little social experimentation. I suspected that by exaggerating the stagger I would be able to observe better the impact that each guest had on the proceedings. So I organized a party and told the first guests to arrive at 1.00 p.m., the second at 2.00 p.m., the third at 3.00 p.m., and so on, until 11 p.m. Which meant that each set of guests had a different idea of what kind of party it was. Those who arrived at 1.00 p.m. would probably be expecting something low-key – say, a light buffet and a bottle of Cava – while the three o'clock arrivals might reasonably expect a barbecue. The seven o'clock guests might think that they had been "invited to dinner", and would continue to labour under this misapprehension until nine, when those who had been told to come in fancy dress rolled up. And these sailors, centurions and pirates, these Lord Nelsons, Rasputins and Mussolinis, would themselves be trumped by those who had been told simply to come round when the pubs shut in their civilian clothing. I will not bore you with the specific observations that this approach afforded (the truth was, any anthropological insight was compromised by my guests' failure to show at the anticipated hour – for I had forgotten, when preparing this timetable, to allow for the very lateness that had engendered it), but the one thing I did notice was that a guest's *departure* would have far greater impact than their arrival. Clearly I had been implementing the precise opposite of the experiment I should have been conducting, and I lost no time in repeating the entire process, this time asking guests to *leave* rather than arrive at a specific time.

I discovered that assembling everyone I knew and then gradually removing certain people from the equation was a far more effective way of getting the social blend *just right*. To use a sculptural analogy, I was a better carver than a modeller, finding it easier to subtract rather than add material. And I was an impatient crafts-man too. Instead of wasting valuable time putting tim-id guests at their ease, or perhaps introducing them to more voluble guests whose towering anecdotes would afford ample refuge, I would cordially request that they leave immediately, often employing jocular euphemisms like "I think you should take an early bath", or managerial terminology like "I'm going to have to let you go". While it is true that I encouraged timid or taciturn guests to keep their coats on, I did stress that the social dynamic of any given night would not necessarily be the template for future ones: those asked to leave early on one occasion were reassured that they might perform a more instrumental role, if not the next time, then certainly the time after that.

There were subsequent, less successful experiments, but this – I now see in retrospect – was the genesis of my current applications procedure. We now move on to consider how my gradual ostracism by my *existing* friends led to the rubric for obtaining *new* ones, for I did say that the former had engendered the latter.

After these experiments, I entered into lengthy correspondence with my disgruntled friends – and not just with those who had played only ancillary roles at my gatherings (and who still attended in the hope of enjoying a much longer "stay at the crease"), but with those who had stormed out in protest at another's expulsion. The exchanges with these friends were more profound than any "amicable" face-to-face conversations we had ever had. Issues were aired that had never been broached before. It seemed to me that friendship prospered through conflict, whereas harmony stunted its growth. Admittedly, this was an opinion that, when communicated in a letter to several long-standing companions, invariably had the effect of killing a friendship. But before the friendship died, it usually yielded – in its final contortions – corroboration of the following fact: that what people hide in person they reveal in correspondence. Distance, it seems, affords greater intimacy than face-to-face conversation. This is unsurprising, as many of the things that people say to one another in person are, I'm afraid, simply an attempt to avoid silence. Silence emphasizes the interlocutors' bodily presence, leading to mutual discomfort; they start fidgeting, their fingers drum the table as their minds wander – wander so far that they ask themselves why their bodies have not followed, why, in short, they are still *here*. Ninety percent of the time conversation is nothing more than a distraction from the embarrassment of having company, of having another actual human being there in front of you. The greatest friends are those with whom one can enjoy a lengthy silence, to whom silence is as important as speech: to whom speech is not the avoidance of silence but a method of navigating it, of bringing about *different kinds* of silence. For silence has an unacknowledged and instrumental diversity. The silence that follows a faux pas is different to that which precedes a bon mot; the silence in between each piece of dialogue in a play, though not "scripted", is – as champions of Pinter are fond of remarking – as integral to its dramatic effect as the words that fall from the protagonists' mouths. That the silence is animated only by what is said *after* it does not lessen its effect or importance.

But this is a digression. Suffice to say that for a long time I would never actually meet with friends in person: friendship was restricted entirely to correspondence. The need to "initiate corporeal verification"[1] was first mooted a decade ago by a new recruit who has since graduated to what I suppose passes in my circle for a "soulmate". No sooner had I taken this fellow on, than he began recommending some adjustments to the protocol I had employed in the preceding years, the most radical of which was that I should meet each friend annually. It is as well I consented to this, for after three years of corporeal verification I suspected some individuals of passing themselves off as others, and some of multiple noms de plume. A further two years confirmed what the soulmate had suspected all along: that the "forty" correspondents

1.   S. Ashton, 'When and Why We Meet', *Friendship Prospectus 2012–13*, p. 4.

were in fact fifteen in number, that I had fewer friends than I thought – news I did not greet with the dismay one might have expected. On the contrary, I was elated: how kind of my friends to adopt alter egos merely to give me an inflated sense of my own popularity.

But the main purpose in meeting friends annually is simply to find out who has died and who still exists. The sadness at one friend's death is offset by the exciting prospect of another stepping into the breach as a "surrogate", picking up where the previous incumbent left off. My friends had already initiated this process informally by adopting alter egos, and on the advice of my soulmate I have ratified it as a fundamental paradigm. What matters, after all, is the friendship itself, not the individuals who comprise it. In this sense, death is of little consequence, no more inconvenient than, say, someone handing in their notice at work. However, I am mindful of the fact that, due to my reluctance to terminate any of the forty friendships, the workload of my *extant* friends is increasing with each death. Consequently, there are now more friendships being maintained by fewer people than ever before: another decade and the administration of *all* friendships may lie exclusively in the hands of my soulmate. Though he has professed himself more than equal to the task, I believe that now is the time to increase my intake of friends, for if possible I would like all forty friendships to continue beyond my death. This will, of course, eventually see the soulmate assuming my own role, and appointing his own soulmate, who will in turn succeed him.

Posthumous friendships are an exciting innovation I owe entirely to the vision of my soulmate and heir. Those who implement them will be afforded the unique privilege of continuing friendships they had no part in inaugurating, and their distant successors will, it is hoped, inherit friendships of incredible richness: projects begun centuries ago by long-dead personages whose identity is now not only a mystery but a matter of little importance. I repeat: what matters is the friendship, not the individuals who comprise it. The reader will recall that I mentioned three categories at the outset: acquaintance, correspondence and friendship. It remains only to indicate how they interrelate. Let us deal with these three levels of intimacy in turn, adopting, for a minute, the argot of more conventional human relations. We are all familiar, I hope, with the phrase "Glad to make your acquaintance". Thus, to quote from my prospectus:

> "Your **acquaintance**" is not so much something I am "glad to make" as a state of *reduced hostility*. A **correspondence** occurs when this reduced hostility breaks out into *full-blown tolerance*. A correspondence advances to **friendship** only by attaining a state that renders it worthy of posthumous continuation by subsequent incumbents. In its most general sense, this state can be summarized as one in which the correspondent's sense of "individuality" no longer impedes the efficiency of the social intercourse.

– 214 –

I acknowledge that the reader may see little difference between "correspondence" and "friendship" here, inasmuch as the latter brooks minimal corporeal verification and the former none whatsoever. In Part II it will become clearer how promotion from the one to the other is achieved within the protocols described above.

I look forward to "renewing our acquaintance" in the spring volume of this journal.

– *The European Sociological Review*, 2013

Sustainable Forest

On Tuesday the nation voted for the first recipient of the Eduardo Paolozzi Award. It is unusual for the public to be given the opportunity to adjudicate on matters of high culture, but in this case entirely appropriate, since the award is for the best public artwork of the last decade.

The inauguration of the Paolozzi – which seeks to emulate the prestigious Münster Sculpture Project, now in its fourth decade – has not been without its problems. I refer not just to the proposed infrequency of the award (once every decade makes it a too significant cultural barometer) or to the alleged decision to veto national monuments, but to the nature of the judging process. The steering committee's initial plan was to assemble a panel of connoisseurs from several artistic fields. However, when the Minister for Culture intervened earlier in the year to question the wisdom of giving an award for best public artwork without including the public in the decision-making process, everything changed. The tabloid media, ever alive to the political pressure points of high culture, drew attention to the "vast amount of taxpayers' money" expended on most of the shortlisted works, and applied its customary Vulcan death grip. The committee's hand was forced, and in a mere three months what had begun as a somewhat marginal event played out behind closed doors took on an altogether more populist aspect.

When it comes to the popularization of high culture, it is surprising how often it is that only tabloid disdain attracts the attention of television producers – and this case has been no different. When Channel 4 stepped in with an offer to cover the Paolozzi, many feared it would go the same way as the Turner Prize. However, Optomen, the production company commissioned to produce *The Nation's Favourite Public Artwork*, have somehow managed to avoid accusations of dumbing down – despite the fact that their involvement has seen the more elitist members of the Paolozzi's steering committee jettisoned in favour of more egalitarian "consultants". Their two-part programme, though marred by the usual interjections from professional talking heads and by torrents of crass jingoism from "controversial" cultural firebrands, is on the whole both informed and accessible, contextualizing the shortlisted works within a concise history of public art in diligent fashion. In part one, presented by Griff Rhys Jones, ten celebrities were invited to put the case for their favourite work. The public were then invited to vote by telephone and text message to reduce this number to a shortlist of four. In part two, presented by Jools Holland, they were asked to vote for an outright winner.

They chose *Sustainable Forest* by Tim Bailey. There has been bemusement from both elitist and populist quarters that they did not plump for one of the more "spectacular" works, i.e. for Antony Gormley's *Angel of the North*, Thomas Heatherwick's *B of the Bang* or Marc Quinn's *Alison Lapper Pregnant*. These pieces have featured regularly on the "…and finally" addenda of national news bulletins and need no introduction, whereas the eventual winner was virtually unknown before the Channel 4 programme was broadcast.

Sustainable Forest was an off-site contribution to the 2004 exhibition *Freehouse* at the MOT gallery in London. Located in the Hare, a pub on nearby Cambridge Heath Road, it was intended as a temporary work but has since become a standard fixture, blending so seamlessly with its surroundings as to invite attention from perhaps only one in every hundred drinkers. A framed brown parchment of handwritten text, it resembles the kind of thing we might find in any East End pub. Such objects tend to fall into two categories: those that have hung there for decades as a testament to the history of the immediate locale – engravings depicting railway construction or shipyards, for example – and those that have the appearance of "curiosities" introduced by new landlords eager to assert their proprietary authorship.

Sustainable Forest falls somewhere between the two – for what initially appears to be a drab historical document is subsequently discovered to be an outlandish curiosity. It takes the form of a nineteenth-century manumission paper, the aggressively slanted and almost illegible script lending convincing authenticity. Only on a third viewing did I verify the document as apocryphal. Had I been sober enough on my previous two visits to make it to the end of the first meandering sentence –

Pleas at the Court House in Corbin County, and the State of Kentucky, of the Corbin County Probate Court, within and for said County, at a session thereof held at the place aforesaid on the fifteenth day of October…

– I would have noticed that it is not a genuine manumission paper but a doctored facsimile. A more diligent (that is to say, sober) critic, on completing the document's opening sentence, would have noted that the executor of the emancipation was one "Colonel Harland Sanders", the founder of KFC, while a still more diligent one would have established the identity of the slave owner as "Walt Disney of Orlando, and the State of Florida", who,

in consideration of one dollar paid to me, and for my other good and sufficient considerations, before these present, emancipate and set free my slave, Britney Spears.

On the one hand, as a public artwork *Sustainable Forest* is resolutely inconspicuous: unlike Gormley's, Quinn's and Heatherwick's pieces, it does not militate bombastically for our attention by dominating its context, but is content to wait its turn alongside the ordinary matter that surrounds it. However, *informationally* it is as conspicuous as can be. To the surprised few who do notice it, it becomes every bit as dominant as *Angel of the North* or *B of the Bang* (if not quite as controversial as *Alison Lapper Pregnant*). Moreover, the surprise of this minority is amplified by the suspicion that most people have *not* noticed it. Its appeal as public art, in other words, lies in its refusal to declare itself to all-comers, its refusal to earmark "the public" as a single homogeneous entity. Perhaps this is why they voted for it on Tuesday.

– *The Plastic Arts*, 2005

Heaven's Anus

The following article was my last act as Vicar of Wroxham, a post I held from 2010 to 2013.

I was sorry to learn that my sermon on Sunday 10th August did not meet with universal approval. Indeed, I must infer from the silence of my family and friends, and from the divorce proceedings initiated by my wife, that it did not even meet with the *particular* approval of my nearest and dearest. Nevertheless, I would like, in the pages of this, the *East Wroxham & District Parish Newsletter*, to reiterate the divine knowledge vouchsafed to me in a vision and relayed to you all two weeks ago from the pulpit of St Mary's: that it is not Man's mortal conduct on Earth that determines his fitness to stand at God's side for all eternity, but his conduct in Heaven that determines his right to take his place on Earth. We have laboured under a staggering misapprehension: in the shape of the scriptures of bygone epochs, Man has built a telescope of astonishing theological perspicacity, a veritable Hubble designed to shorten the distance between himself and God – and has gazed unflinchingly through the wrong end of it for more than two millennia. A hackneyed metaphor, you might think, but I can think of no clearer indication of the extent of the Great Theological Error, which I will repeat more plainly for the slow-witted: it is not those on Earth who enter Heaven, but those in Heaven who come to Earth.

Initially, when Jesus gathered me up and took me beyond the cosmos, where there is neither time nor space, I confess I thought he had come to set my soul before God. "Ah, I have passed away in my sleep," I said to myself with some relief (for I had always feared meeting my end through sudden and brutal means). But it became apparent that I was still very much alive and not in fact about to receive Divine Judgement. No, I was not here to throw off the lineaments of my earthly existence and enter a state of disembodied immortality; on the contrary, my stay in Heaven was to be brief, "about as long as it took the Ghost of Christmas Past to show Scrooge the error of his ways," were Jesus's actual words – though he quickly added that it was not specifically my ways but humanity's that he wanted to show me the error of.

Jesus said that I was to be an emissary, that I was to convey to the world's religious leaders the true extent of their misunderstanding: that I was, in short, to be "the prophet to end all prophecy". He then threw open the doors to a space whose vastness can only be conveyed by the following contradiction: it was an interior larger than any exterior I have ever known. It did not *occupy* space; it *was* space: all space. Its ceiling was a stratosphere, while its walls were more distant than any planetary horizon. Its dominion was quite simply beyond spatial assessment – and yet there was the palpable sense of being *inside* it. I turned to Jesus:

"So this is it then: Heaven."

"Heaven as you see it, Anglican," replied Jesus, "Heaven as *you* see it."

"What, you mean… you mean that, that…"

"That it exists in tangible form only insofar as you yourself can imagine it – or, more accurately, as you have already imagined it."

I looked around and saw what I thought were figures, human figures, arrayed in irregular clusters, the sole indication of scale in a context that was apparently without scale. Yes, I had beheld this spectacle before in my mind's eye, perhaps a handful of times, at the oddest and as it were most mundane moments – when paying for a newspaper, say, or scratching an itch. I believe I also glimpsed it once or twice in a sort of half-dream, at that moment just before one falls asleep.

"You must understand," resumed Jesus, "that you are seeing what no other man has seen or ever will see. And because you are seeing what was not intended to be seen by any living thing, what you see makes little sense. Your faculties have constructed an illusion to compensate for their inability to grasp that which is present but not tangible, that which is palpable but not, as it were, "embodied". As an embodied entity forced to exist in time, you cannot *see the potential*.

For Heaven is nothing if not a sea of potentiality. It is not – as Man has hitherto conceived it – an end, or even a beginning, but a prelude to beginning. It is not surprising that, in the face of your inability to perceive this potentiality, you have substituted an illusion, an illusion based on a picture of Heaven that first occurred to you, if I am not mistaken, in a newsagents in Norwich?"

"So it did, so it did. Yes, I remember. It's quite an impressive illusion isn't it? I realize of course that it's not particularly original but—"

"Anglican, you must not, as an embodied mammal, apologize for your inability to conceive of a more fitting context for disembodied existence. Please, do not reproach yourself for summoning an image that approximates to nothing more than a two-star Valhalla. But none of this is germane to our real purpose. Come, I must show you the sea of potentiality. In a moment you will feel rather strange. Do not be alarmed; I am merely recalibrating your being to suit your current circumstances."

And with that the illusory figures evaporated, as did everything given to sensory experience. Jesus and I were subsumed into a single entity, an entity which completely interlaced with our environment – if Heaven can be thus described. Body, mind and space were as one. I neither saw, heard, smelt, tasted nor felt – for the lack of a boundary between body and environment rendered the senses redundant. More-over, there was now no need for Jesus to speak and for me to listen, for there was no separateness between us, no separateness between any individual entities at all, just a continuous spectrum of consciousness. Even then – inveterate pedagogue that I am – it occurred to me that I was going to have some difficulty conveying all this to my congregation on returning to my parish. So I hope you will forgive me for continuing to represent my dialogue with Jesus as an exchange between two corporeally distinct interlocutors, for the process of intuitive apprehension by which we actually communicated would be impossible to transcribe.

The first thing I was keen to discover was why Jesus had waited so long to disabuse Mankind of its theological fallacy. Jesus replied that therein lay a story, and fell into a somewhat morose silence – as though about to disclose something difficult and cathartic. At length he regained his composure:

"It was a regrettable episode, but since it may improve your understanding of the fallacy I suppose I should recount it. I said earlier that no mortal man had gazed upon the sea of potentiality. That was untrue. There is one other who has beheld it, whose being has commingled with my own, as yours is now; a man who, about two and a half thousand years ago, I attempted to engage with the same duties that you will shortly discharge – and, I hope, discharge ably (though to the probable dismay of your scandalized flock). Unfortunately this man, fearing accusations of heresy from his students and peers, misrepresented

what I told him, adding his own rhetorical embellish-
ments."

Jesus then described this "misrepresentation" in
some detail. The terminology used in his account led
me to the conclusion that he could only be talking
about one man, and I could not resist the urge to
splutter his name.

"*Plato?*" The two syllables drew a sharp intake of
breath.

"It was he. I had wanted Aristotle – whose entele-
chal doctrine was to prove more compatible with the
True Theology – but unfortunately he was too young
at the time. So I had to settle for Plato, who put it
about on Earth that... incidentally, Anglican, can I
assume your ecumenical apprenticeship included
some rudimentary grounding in the practice known as
"philosophy"? Good. Then you will know that Plato
considered earthly forms to be "imperfect" versions of
ideal forms that exist outside of space and time. In
order to exist *in* space and time, he said, these forms
have to renounce their ideal state. Thus, the physical
world you call 'Earth' is an imperfect copy..."

"Of an 'archetypal' reality?"

"Please don't interrupt. But yes, of an 'archetypal
reality'. However, the truth is somewhat different,
for the eventual form of the potentialities you see
here, and *here*, and *here*," said Jesus, gesturing at
random nodes on the spectrum of consciousnesses
with maniacal emphasis, "will deviate profoundly
from any such 'ideal' state. Mutation is their natural

prerogative. There is no general 'Platonic Truth' underpinning mortal particularities, no ideal state of being to which things return at their death. Truth is simply a compendium of these particularities. Truth is not the passive metaphysical substrate of all that is, but the active cumulative effect of all that will be. It is an evolving algorithm – a sort of ongoing 'ontological calculation', if you will, with beings and things in place of numbers and symbols. However, with Man this algorithm was always destined to reach a flashpoint. You see, Man has always felt himself to be the *object* of the algorithm, rather than the *modulus* of its evolution."

"The what?"

"The modulus: the constant indicating the relation between a physical effect and its cause. In this case the effect is life, and the cause is divine."

"But by describing this cause as divine you're saying that God is the origin of everything, which surely concurs with Judaeo-Christian theology—"

"I made no mention of any 'God'. There is no such 'author' at large within the spectrum of consciousness, no such harbourmaster patrolling the sea of potentiality. By 'divine' I refer simply to the origin of life, not to any fundamental reason for its existence. The cause-and-effect relation between Heaven and Earth is not supernatural; it is teleological. Everything found in the latter is simply the natural excretive corollary of the former."

"What do you mean, 'excretive'?"

"I repeat: the physical world is not the result of some supernatural deity's magnanimous volition; it is simply the by-product of cosmological potential, a sort of living effluent. Contrary to what your metaphysicians believe, there cannot be an infinite amount of potential. It is finite. Ergo, in order for Heaven – by which I also mean the 'cosmos', incidentally – to accommodate more potential, some of it has to be actualized, that is to say, 'got rid of'. This process, the process by which potential becomes actual, has traditionally been understood by Mankind as the Miracle of Life. In fact it is little more than a kind of bowel movement." Had we been conversing naturally, I would have interrupted Jesus here to point out that, ostensibly, he had just described Earth as a dung heap. But he apprehended my dismay intuitively:

"No, not a dung heap, Anglican, more a sort of… sewage farm." I was surprised at the insensitivity of this remark, and could not help responding flippantly.

"Well, that's OK then. It's a relief to know that life – What did you call it? An 'ontological algorithm'? – is a slightly more sophisticated form of waste-management than I'd initially thought."

"I'll thank you to remember who you're talking to. Sarcasm is not a becoming trait, especially in prophets. But if it helps you to understand it that way, then yes, 'waste management' is a not inapposite description. I am sorry that the 'Truth'" – and here Jesus made the extra-corporeal equivalent of a quote-unquote gesture – "is somewhat less edifying than you envisaged; as a unification of ecological, theological and cosmological principles, I had assumed it would be more palatable – comforting, even. After all, it does not differ greatly from what your Gaia theorists have been telling you for the last fifty years. I believe it was Mr Lovelock who introduced the notion of the Earth as a single, self-regulating organism. Such thinking, of course, does not advance much beyond the observation that the biosphere is subordinate to the ecosphere. As I have pointed out, however, *both* are subordinate to, what shall we call it... a 'potentasphere' – though in a strictly cloacal sense. Surely, you have felt the inherent futility of matter, not least in the wretched inertia of your own flesh, its constant reluctance to comply with your wishes? Has it ever occurred to you that your body would *rather not exist*? Why, it is nothing more than animated ordure.

"Let me come at things from another perspective. As I have said, the ideal state for the cosmos – by which I also mean 'Heaven', remember – is one of pure potential, for by manifesting itself physically it would doom itself – as your thermodynamicists have correctly concluded – to eventual stasis. Better for it to remain eternally 'unproven' than embark on such a pointless odyssey. Plato was right in that there exists some higher metaphysical system, but I assure you that system is far from 'ideal': it is not one of 'archetypes', of which earthly forms are a denigration, and to which such denigrated matter will one day return. Rather, it is characterized by a condition of deliberately unfulfilled desire."

"*Desire?* Forgive my interruption Jesus, but isn't that somewhat anthropocentric?"

"Your willingness to debate the finer points of the True Theology bodes well, Anglican. The phrase was clumsily chosen. By 'unfulfilled desire' I refer to the tendency of the potentasphere to abstain from actualizing any single universe in favour of coveting the tenability of all *possible* universes. Your polymath Leibniz was onto something with his 'possible worlds'. I should've summoned *him* as an emissary, were it not for his ghastly intellectual vanity."

"In summary then, Jesus, the mortal coil is not the redemptive passage we Christians believe it to be?"

"Anglican, how can I put this? Earth is but Heaven's anus, the arse of the universe, an organ of cosmological evacuation. Life may *feel* significant, but it is simply a by-product of, as you put it, 'waste management' on a huge scale: existence is merely the sensation of epochal excretion and decay. The apparent diversity of life is a necessarily complex mechanism: you see, things must decay at different rates for the process of waste management to be tenable over an indefinite period. Hence the need for an ontological algorithm, one that embraces all that you call the kingdoms of plants, insects, mammals, minerals, etc."

"And this is what you told Plato?"

"The very same."

"And how did he respond to this, er, 'divine knowledge'?"

"He had so much difficulty accepting the facts that he invented a scenario whereby the waste could be 'recycled', converted back into 'archetypal Form'. And this distortion – that all things come from an ideal state to which they will eventually return – enabled Christianity to found the notion that the soul is an essence that transcends mortality, and the consequent fallacy that 'truth', 'revelation', call it what you will, is attained only on its rebirth as a disembodied archetype."

"And what did you do, Jesus, on discovering Plato's betrayal?"

At this point Jesus laughed thunderously. "Haha... Sorry, forgive me, but you've reminded me of a saying popular on Earth, often uttered at moments of insoluble moral dilemma. 'What would Jesus do?' you ask yourselves. And here you are, asking Jesus himself what he actually did, totally oblivious to the irony! Well, I'll tell you what Jesus did. *Jesus wept*. That's what he did. Wept. For there followed two thousand years of inconsequential Bible-bashing and numerous wars fought on the most trivial pretexts. For the first time in eternity – if you will forgive the oxymoron – I was moved to consider Man as something more than mere effluent, and I felt pity for him, so alone in the universe. I wept at the Crusades and the Inquisition, at the asinine brutality of it all, cursing Plato all the time. Only now have I summoned the courage to seek another emissary."

SEAN ASHTON

"And why... why *me*?"

"Simple. You lack faith. More specifically, you lack just the right amount of faith, and in just the right areas, to be susceptible to the True Theology."

What Jesus meant by this is still not entirely clear to me. I let it pass, for I had more pressing enquiries. You will recall what I said at the outset: that it is not Man's mortal conduct on Earth that determines his fitness to stand beside God for all eternity, but his conduct in Heaven that determines his right to take his mortal place on this Earth. On reflection, my congregation was right to question the use of that word 'conduct' to describe a process in which conventional notions of embodiment – conception, gestation, birth and corporeal existence – are subsumed under the wider cosmological imperative of being shat randomly through Heaven's anus. Jesus had put considerable spin on things with his "ontological algorithms" and so forth, but no amount of jargon could disguise the facts, and I was keen for some direction as to how best to convey to the world's religious leaders what he had told me. Alas, no such advice was forthcoming; I could feel my consciousness returning to its body; evidently Jesus felt his work was done, and his words faded as he extricated himself from his newly appointed prophet:

"Tell them the unvarnished truth, Anglican," he said, as we drifted apart, "for you have gleaned all you need to do my bidding on Earth, and it is time to set you back down in England..."

* * *

And so it was that I came to, in St Mary's at eleven o'clock on Sunday 10th August, gripping the sides of my pulpit and staring into a hundred faces. By placing me there, Jesus knew that I would have no time to reflect on what he had said or on the repercussions of relaying it to the world. He knew also that I had prepared nothing to say to you that morning, and that consequently I would have either to stand in awkward silence for the duration of my sermon or launch immediately into an account of what I had just witnessed.

I chose the latter.

– *East Wroxham & District Parish Newsletter*, 2013

Brick Lane Market Revisited

Brick Lane Market has changed. The number of people selling superannuated crap for a pittance has dwindled. The "ghostly facilitators of mercantile entropy" mentioned in my previous article have become exactly that – ghosts haunting the margins of the market, where Cheshire Street meets Vallance Road. Here they continue to hawk their wares, their Moulinex Blender manuals, SodaStream gas canisters, Wimpy condiment dispensers, rain-soaked Bontempi keyboards and Elizabeth Duke jewellery. But for how much longer? Am I alone in feeling that the nearby Sunday Upmarket complex, which accommodates stallholders displaced by the ongoing redevelopment of Spitalfields Market, is beginning to influence Brick Lane Market for the worse? Are my fears that Brick Lane's superannuated crap will soon give way to Chinese slippers, dreamcatchers, moon calendars and quaint wooden toys aimed at children who exist only in the imagination of Enid Blyton – are these fears justified?[1]

---

1. Or am I just being reactionary? After all, not everything has changed: pornographers continue to prosper, and it is still possible for cyclists to have their bikes stolen and sold back to them within the hour.

It's easy to sneer at the vacuous alterity of such products, but perhaps we should try to regard it with the same spirit of anthropological curiosity that we brought to bear on the "entrepreneurial witchcraft of London's desperately poor" eight years ago (*The Sardinian*, November 1999). Readers will recall that the subject of my previous article was an indigent underclass who believed that extant matter in any form could be not only commodified but used "liturgically" in a ritual of self-affirmation. This ritual, though undertaken without aesthetic intention, often engendered tableaux of a highly aesthetic and symbolic nature: centimes dropped casually into an ashtray became a pithy commentary on French Europhilia; Hoover attachments laid out on blankets resembled a decommissioned paramilitary-arms cache ("weapons of mess extraction", a friend once quipped). The appeal of these tableaux lies in their sheer inadvertency, their authors effectively a movement of idiot-savant sculptors. Their *faux*hemi-an pretenders, by contrast, convinced that "everyone is an artist" and deserves the chance to peddle their art on the open market, seem to exercise an excess of aesthetic will. In so doing they demonstrate complete aesthetic impoverishment. The aesthetics they deploy are impoverished for reasons too numerous to list here, but mainly because they are constrained by the limited commodificational formats of the marketplace – whereas their indigent precursors see the commodity as a form as mutable as matter itself. The difference between the *faux*hemians and the indigents could not be clearer: the former begs you to buy, the latter *dares* you to buy.

My recent anthropological enquiries were conducted in the belief – or was it the hope? – that the two positions were not mutually exclusive. As Sir Clive Sinclair once noted, the best cure for nostalgia is to not only embrace change but become its *agency*, and thereby distract oneself from the losses it must necessarily entail.

I took the plunge and wangled a pitch in the Sunday Upmarket complex. My business venture took various forms during the six months it lasted, but there is space enough here to describe only the two most successful. I began by selling clothes. I had been intrigued, during the years that had passed since my first article on Brick Lane Market and the present one, by the proliferation of retro clothes shops in the area. What interested me was the gradual blurring of the distinction between the terms "retro" and "used" – which I date from around 1995, when all those shell suits that had been so stigmatized by Loadsamoney, Guru Josh and David Icke and that had steadily clogged the rails of Oxfam and Cancer Research began, incredibly, to be sold as "retro". The so-bad-it's-good principle that began with the redemption of the shell suit and culminated in the restitution of the mullet also encompassed, albeit briefly, such maligned labels as British Home Stores, C&A, Littlewoods and Fosters Menswear, a handful of fashionistas incorporating the odd jumper from these stores into an ironic "geek" look. Had it not eschewed the period 1987–90 – surely the worst in the history of British knitwear design – this particular look might have had greater mileage, but in opting for a slightly earlier period it was lumped in with the wider, ongoing revisitation of mid-Eighties casual. Fosters Menswear in particular produced some *sui generis* pieces during this period, many of which, strangely, seemed to end up in eastern Europe. Thus, the first Balkan refugees to arrive in the UK in the mid-Nineties were dressed in a style that had not long fallen from British high-street favour.[2]

Now we all know how fashion loves an outfit to tell a story. And here, surely, was a story. I say "surely" – as though the reader has the faintest idea what I'm talking about. Let me explain. During World War II the British government had been a patsy in Josip Tito's bid for Partisan supremacy over the Chetniks in Yugoslavia: in 1943 Tito deceived Churchill into believing that the Chetniks were German collaborators, and Allied aid was swiftly transferred to the Partisans. The Partisans then used Allied munitions against the Chetniks in a merciless campaign, eventually establishing a post-war Communist government, sowing the seeds of future Balkan unrest by creating the "powder keg" state in which ethnic discord was to remain bottled up for fifty years before being so brutally vented in the early Nineties. The notion of injudicious foreign policy

---

2. Former Manchester United and England captain Bryan Robson was a noted exponent of this style. He boasted an extraordinary range of knitwear, favouring the kind of jumpers that most men will only wear on Christmas morning.

having later repercussions is hardly a new one, but in this case it was not so much the circuitous connection between past political oversight and future human catastrophe that intrigued me as the particular tableau which evoked it. It came hobbling towards me along the desolate promenade of Hastings seafront one November afternoon, chest ablaze with the kind of video feedback that can only be the product of late-Eighties British knitwear design. It sounds absurd, I know, to say that an acrylic jumper from Fosters Menswear awakened my political conscience, and had the man in question been wearing something slightly more recent I might never have made the connection. As it was, his attire crystallized it for me instantly: what better way of seeking refuge in a country which had inadvertently seeded political unrest in his own than by sporting garments from its worst sartorial period in living memory?

My 'Asylum-Seeker Chic' spread appeared in the very next issue of *Vice* magazine, and the look – flammable knitwear, steel crutches, frosted denim jeans with elasticated bottoms – was widely emulated in Shoreditch. I made a killing buying up the very worst in British fashion on eBay for a song and flogging it on my stall for a musical. While mainstream fashion has yet to be affected, Brick Lane, as ever, provides the blueprint that high-street designers will undoubtedly follow. Champions of the old Brick Lane will recall that the asylum-seeker look was exemplified by the many immigrant black marketeers that once plied their trade there. Indeed, some still do, and when I recently learnt of incidents of contraband tobacconists mistaking groups of Hoxtonites for rival gangs muscling in on their patch, I smiled with the satisfaction of one who knows his work is done.

By the time the recriminations began, my stall had changed into a food outlet. I had always eyed the surrounding food outlets with a certain envy, boasting as they did the lucrative provenance of "authentic ethnic cuisine". But being English, white and from Essex, joining the ranks of these was not going to be easy. What would I cook? I'd never liked pie and mash – and anyway that was cockney fare. I briefly considered seafood – but was soon talked out of it by a persuasive acquaintance of the Aldgate-based jellied-eel specialist, Tubby Isaacs. This left either fish 'n' chips or roast beef and Yorkshire pud, both of which seemed somewhat reactionary compared to the exotic fare offered by others.

I ditched my plans for authentic English cuisine at the last minute, selling jacket potatoes as a stopgap measure that first week. Thanks to my formal training as a sculptor at the Royal College of Art under Professor Glynn Williams, I was able to offer not only potatoes in their jackets, but potatoes in their vests and underpants. This gimmick momentarily deflected attention from my culinary shortcomings, but as the day wore on the ethnic neutrality of my cuisine became a talking point among the other stallholders.

The competitive camaraderie among whom, I might add, was augmented by the fact that each flew the flag of their national cuisine. Now you see why my belief in English cuisine had quickly faltered, for I could hardly fly the inflammatory St George's Cross. Had I adopted a "fusion" style of cooking, I would doubtless have hoisted the Jolly Roger in playful recognition of that cuisine's piratical initiative. But even this seemed outmoded – and classically English in its studied self-marginalization. I thought about adopting the cuisine of a tiny nation like the Faroe Islands, but the acquisition of the ingredients required to make the national dishes and the research necessary to cook them proved prohibitive. A third option was the invention of a fictional cuisine, which of course entailed imagining a new country and race of people. Those weeks when my stall underwent a transition from one product to another were hectic enough, and in this particular week there was scarcely time to lay my hands on any produce, let alone formulate the cultural back story required to fashion it into an apocryphal cuisine.

Then I remembered that for her 2001 show at Camden Arts Centre the artist Sophie Calle had, at the suggestion of the author Paul Auster, consumed meals of a single colour at set times of the day for one week; and that the sculptor Franz West had in 1998 exhibited a gourdlike object filled with whisky from which viewers were invited to drink. Both of these ideas had appealed to my interest in the "objecthood" of food – how it comes, the shape and weight of it, the feel of it in the hand, the haptic appraisal of nourishment – and so, short of other ideas, I decided to develop these interests into a sort of "ergonomic tapas".

My early experiments were fairly conservative, amounting to nothing more than an expansion of samosa triangularity – for centuries the province of equilateralism – to include isosceles and scalene variations. The subtlety of which, sadly, was lost on most customers. Not until the third week did my speculations begin to embrace the *portability* of food. My monogrammed chapatis that could be folded into the breast pocket of a suit; my nan breads with spiral mince designs that produced pleasing optical effects when used as frisbees; my "wraps" that were, basically, edible pass-the-parcels to be eaten communally to musical accompaniment – these were all elaborations of standard fare, extending the concept of portability into *application*. Most food sold at the market was, as you'd expect, intended for ambulatory consumption; I stole a march on my competitors by offering things intended for supine, prone and pendent consumption – liquorice, mostly. There was also a brief dalliance with straightforwardly figurative forms (a chess set made from truffles so irresistible as to encourage positionally compromising pawn exchanges was consumed in minutes), but it was only a matter of time before my innovations lurched into the area of metaphysics. Certain foods have long been attributed extra-nutritive powers (e.g. aphrodisiacal), and of course the sacrament entails nothing less than the transubstantiation of commonplace victuals into Christ's body and blood.

This idea of changing the substance of a thing without changing its outward appearance suggested a gap in the market for one who was becoming bored with the whole morphology of food. Thus it was that, when administered in conjunction with a prescribed versicle, my chipolatas *became* the dicks of minor actors; my sweetmeats, unless consumed while sprinting along a particular Norfolk bridleway reciting the fourth canto of Ezra Pound's *Homage to Sextus Propertius*, bestowed no nourishment whatsoever; and as for my misfortune cookies, well, they drove my neighbour, a freelance horoscopist, to distraction. I also offered things that might be eaten in principle, if not in practice – oh, and hot cakes that helped fight the war against terror.

The attribution of metaphysical properties to routine foodstuffs was in retrospect a symptom of my increasing boredom with the ornate morphology of food preparation, which is after all, as Dr Johnson once observed, "a grandiose deferral of its excremental destiny" or "shit waiting to happen", as Will Self more candidly put it two centuries later. Thanks to the loan of the Belgian artist Wim Delvoye's *Cloaca* (a machine that converts edible matter into faecal matter), the food I sold during my final month at the Sunday Upmarket complex looked *exactly* like shit. Of course, *Cloaca* had to be recalibrated to produce only the *appearance* of shit, the harmful toxins being removed at the final stage of production. Food purchased from other outlets provided the raw material: Stilton-and-broccoli quiche, focaccia with sun-dried tomato, tartine of confit onion with smoked ham and numerous other dishes were fed into a garbage-disposal unit, where they were mechanically masticated into boluses that were sent on a "digestive" odyssey through six vats connected by pipes, tubes and pumps (the collective equivalent of the stomach, pancreas and intestines) at a precise temperature of 37.2°C, and eventually extruded onto plates carried via a conveyor belt to the customer seating area, which was arranged around *Cloaca* in a manner reminiscent of a sushi bar. As I had envisaged, this reassuring resemblance to a familiar dining format, and the equally reassuring technical complexity of Delvoye's device led most customers to conclude that what they were eating was not in fact detoxified shit but some kind of weird, probably soya-based, concoction.

Earlier I accused the *faux*hemians of compromising their wares by accepting the commodificational limitations of the marketplace, and championed the indigent's ability to see the commodity as a form as mutable as matter itself. Whether any of the forms that my own stall assumed managed to reconcile these two approaches is not for me to judge, but I think I proved that the *faux*hemian's homespun alterity and gratuitous over-invention can, if pushed far enough, create its own unique market. The *faux*hemian is neoterically inventive. I too was neoterically inventive. But my invention had none of the desperation of *faux*hemian commerce: like that of the indigent, it dared rather than begged people to buy. And they did – as long as I kept changing the product, as long as I maintained the impression that my constantly mutating merchandise was in search of an ideal state, a meta-product, if you will.

– *The Sardinian*, 2007

The Vicious Companions Club

Minutes of the Vicious Companions Club Executive Committee Meeting, held on Wednesday 17th March 1992, in Chyde Community Centre, Chyde

Present:

Alan Carter (VCC President; Chair), Geoff Cockshott (Treasurer), Valerie Demeter (Vice President), Judith Pearson (Tippington Choral Society), Ian Lavender (Rotary Club Chyde/Tippington), Kenneth Renton (President, Chyde Art Club), Sean Ashton (Secretary)

1. Apologies for Absence

Michael Hewitt (Vice President, Tippington Round Table; Town Crier, Chyde), Hilary D'Eath (Media Officer, Soroptimist International; VCC Events Organizer), Mr Syncock (Verger, St Matthew's Church, Chyde)

2. Declarations of Interest

There were no declarations of interest from those present at the VCC Executive Committee Meeting. However,

SEAN ASHTON

prior to the meeting, Mr Syncock had instructed
Judith Pearson to notify the Chair of the reasons for his
absence. In Mr Syncock's opinion his attendance would
place pressure on the Committee to rule in favour of his
proposal that his "Wednesdays" should *not* be changed to
another day of the week to accommodate the Tippington
Society of Friends' weekly forum, since the many leaflets
Mr Syncock had taken the time and trouble to design
and photocopy already bore the word "Wednesday". Mr
Syncock also told Mrs Pearson to inform the Committee
that he was "outraged, outraged" at proposals to scrap
the "Over-Nineties Club". Mrs Pearson said that she *had*
pointed out to Mr Syncock that, due to Mrs Derringer's
recent suicide, he was now the only resident of Chyde
and its environs aged 90 or over. In that case, Mr Syncock
had replied, in light of his forthcoming 100th birthday
("only a year and two months away") the "Over-Nineties
Club" might be relaunched as the "Chyde Centenarians
Society" – notwithstanding Mrs Pearson's point that
there were no more residents of Chyde and its environs
aged 100 or over than aged ninety or over. Nevertheless,
concluded Mrs Pearson – despite Ian Lavender's
interjection that they should really move on – Mr Syncock
hoped the Chair would see fit to add the proposal of a
"Chyde Centenarians Society" to the agenda, and that
Mr Syncock's vested interest in this matter be accepted
as further extenuation of his absence from the VCC
Executive Committee Meeting. The Chair decided
that the retention of Mr Syncock's "Wednesdays",
Mr Syncock's outrage at proposals to scrap the

"Over-Nineties Club" and Mr Syncock's counter proposal of a "Chyde Centenarians Society" could all be
added to the agenda of the VCC Executive Committee
Meeting without seriously jeopardizing the likelihood of
their all making it home in time for *Property Ladder*.

3. Matters Arising

3.1 The retention of Mr Syncock's "Wednesdays"

Alan Carter reassured an angry Ian Lavender that
his decision to begin the meeting with those matters
arising directly from Declarations of Interest was
motivated by reasons of pragmatism, for surely it made
sense to discuss the matters relating to Mr Syncock
while they were still fresh in everyone's minds. Ian
Lavender conceded that, though Alan Carter was
clearly an imbecile invested arbitrarily with powers
ratified by no municipal authority, he was quite right
that the freshness of these matters in the minds of the
Committee Members *would* allow them to be dealt
with more efficiently. Ian Lavender then moved that
all Mr Syncock's "Wednesdays" be cut from the VCC
calendar forthwith. When putting this motion to the
Committee, Alan Carter asked the Members to bear
in mind that since Mr Syncock was "not long for this
world" his opportunity for future redress would be
slim – especially if his milkman could be persuaded
to increase the dosage of arsenic that he had been
paying him to syringe through the foil-topped milk

bottles Mr Syncock insisted on and whose tampered-with condition he attributed to blue tits. At this point the President tapped his nose with his finger, a gesture that was interpreted by the other Committee members to mean that he, Alan Carter, would take care of Mr Syncock. The motion was carried. ACTION: AC.

3.2 Mr Syncock's outrage at proposals to scrap the "Over-Nineties Club"

It was agreed that Mr Syncock's outrage at proposals to scrap the "Over-Nineties Club" would be addressed as a consequence of measures stated in item 3.1.

3.3 Mr Syncock's counter-proposal of a "Chyde Centenarians Society"

The Committee was on the verge of unanimously dismissing this proposal when Kenneth Renton made an innovative suggestion. He persuaded the Committee that Mr Syncock "should have his 'Centenarians Society'", under the secret proviso that he be its only elected member (any other centenarians moving into the area being required to live in Chyde for five years to become eligible). In the next two months, expanded Kenneth Renton, due to the inevitable disorientation brought about by measures stated in item 3.1, Mr Syncock might be persuaded to believe that he was a year older than he actually was, allowing the VCC to bring forward the inauguration of the "Chyde Centenarians Society" by a year, to a date that Mr Syncock believed would be his 100th birthday. "It would be expedient to do so," concluded Kenneth Renton, "that we might jettison this old bag of pus by lacing his champagne with a final, lethal dose of poison and toasting his death." ACTION: KR

3.4 Matters concerning the poisoning of Mr Syncock

Although she was the only Committee Member to vote against lethally poisoning Mr Syncock, Valerie Demeter said that it would be remiss of her as a former Senior Lecturer in Organic Chemistry at Birkbeck University not to ask whether they had really "thought this through", pointing out that arsenic was a somewhat inefficient poison, good at killing people gradually over a long period but – unless consumed in large and therefore conspicuous doses – not good for killing people "there and then". Ian Lavender suggested they use mercury. Valerie Demeter replied that unless combined with other chemicals to produce a salt – say, mercury chloride – the insolubility of this heavy liquid metal might present logistical problems. Alan Carter asked Valerie Demeter if she could produce such a compound. Valerie Demeter said that she could probably acquire the necessary components and equipment without having to give anyone her credit-card details, but that in her opinion mercury chloride, though lethal, would not bring about instantaneous death. She elaborated that the victim, on swallowing this salt, would immediately experience acute stomach cramps and a metallic taste in the mouth, followed quickly by bloody vomiting and diarrhoea. Rapid kidney malfunction would then result in an inability to pass urine. Death *can* occur after as little as an hour from a large dose, said Valerie Demeter, but the victim is more likely to succumb to exhaustion 24–48 hours later – which, unfortunately, would give the authorities ample time to question Mr Syncock as his vital organs failed one by one. Alan Carter said that they could not countenance the idea of using mercury chloride. Valerie Demeter offered to undertake further research in this area and to notify the Committee Members as soon as she had decided what would be the most effective substance. Drawing the Committee's attention to the inevitable autopsy that would be conducted on Mr Syncock's body, Valerie Demeter said that it would be helpful to know whether Mr Syncock were being prescribed digitalis for his heart condition, since a quantity 3 or 4 times the prescribed dosage of this drug can be fatal – and might easily be put down to nonagenarian oversight. Ian Lavender thought he could get this information from his wife, a General Practitioner at Tippington Surgery. ACTION: VD, IL.

4. Community Events

4.1 Coffee morning at Chyde Assembly Rooms

The coffee morning at Chyde Assembly Rooms raised £173.

4.2 Forthcoming Lent Supper

Valerie Demeter reported that arrangements for the forthcoming Lent Supper were well in hand. Fifty residents had already made reservations and it was suggested that this number might increase greatly should the VCC be able to secure the John Selwyn Gummer Banqueting Suite at the George Hotel, which holds ninety. Hilary D'Eath's business and political connections have paid off yet again: Neil Hamilton, the newly appointed Minister for Deregulation and Corporate Affairs, has accepted an invitation and agreed to say a few words after dinner on the theme of voluntary repatriation of non-white immigrants. Strangely, no response has yet been received from the Lord Mayor or the Chairman of the Parish Council, despite news of the celebrity guest. It was agreed that we should look for maximum publicity for the event. As Town Crier, Michael Hewitt has already agreed to assist with this. ACTION: VD, MH, HD?

4.3 Use of the recreation ground for the Midsummer Fête

Geoff Cockshott reported that he had secured the use of the recreation ground for the Midsummer Fête.

4.4 Matters concerning Hilary D'Eath's business and political connections

Rising abruptly to his feet, Kenneth Renton launched a frontal attack on Hilary D'Eath, ascribing her regular absence from VCC Executive Meetings to her "haughty assumption that her duties as Media Officer of Soroptimist International had primacy over her duties as VCC Events Organizer". Mr Renton spoke in heated fashion for several minutes, jabbing a finger at Hilary D'Eath's empty chair and stating that "her ability to secure the occasional celebrity guest" was *not* a valid excuse for her absence. Mr Renton moved that, as soon as the Minister for Deregulation and Corporate Affairs Neil Hamilton had RSVPd to their invitation to the Lent Supper, Hilary D'Eath be stripped of her executive status and forbidden to attend meetings for a period of one year. Valerie Demeter calmly advised that they should "field this hot potato with great care". While she was in agreement that the "junketing bitch was clearly taking the piss by lording it up in London on VCC expenses under the pretence of establishing influential metropolitan connections", it was important to handle this affair as politically as possible. What was required, she suggested, was some kind of "unforeseen personal crisis" that would make it impossible for Ms D'Eath to undertake further VCC duties in the immediate future. Ian Lavender agreed that this was a "fantastic" idea and offered to shoot her horses. ACTION: IL, KR, VD.

5. Excursions and Activities

Of the many recent excursions, Geoff Cockshott singled out the trip to Beaconsfield Model Village and the inaugural "Exchange Visit" to Chieveley Good

Companions Club. He also praised Ian Lavender's organization of the "Fathers Afield" initiative (see Item 5.3)

5.1 Geoff Cockshott's "Exchange Visit" to Chieveley Good Companions Club.

In his report of the week he spent with Members of Chieveley Good Companions Club in nearby Chieveley, Geoff Cockshott wrote:

On Monday we were entertained by Mrs Sybil Ratchett and her accordion, with Mr Jynx accompanying on tuba. They played many popular tunes including 'Bananas in Pyjamas' and the 'Chatanooga Choo Choo', encouraging audience participation. Mrs Burrows, the President, proposed a vote of thanks on behalf of the Members. I was given the opportunity to say a few words about how grateful I was to be attending this event, and about how I looked forward with great anticipation to all the other activities that had been organized to coincide with my stay. I also told the Members that I would be fascinated to know what my counterpart was up to in Chyde. On Tuesday we listened with fascination to Mr Reginald Davis's talk about his service with the Home Guard during WWII. Mrs Davis, Mr Davis's wife, operated the slide projector, which at one point broke down! During the forced intermission we were regaled by Ned Quince's tales of poaching and living off the land during the post-war rationing years. On Wednesday we attended an exhibition of needlecraft by Mrs Rosemary Brewning. It included a crocheted skirt and many petticoats. Members found these most interesting. They also found the sketches quite interesting, though not as interesting as the petticoats. On Thursday I was taken to Chieveley Winter Gardens, which were delightful. I was sorry to leave my new friends on Friday – but not before being entertained by amateur prestidigitator Mr Malcolm Jeffries during a farewell luncheon at the Blue Lion Inn. His close-up magic is really quite impressive.

Geoff Cockshott then asked if anyone had "seen hide or hair" of the "counterpart" referred to in his report. Members of the Committee said they did not know that he, Geoff Cockshott, had even made this arrangement with Chieveley Good Companions Club. Geoff Cockshott drew their attention to Item 4.2 of the February Executive Committee Meeting of the VCC, which stated clearly that a Mr David Lucas would be arriving at Chyde Station on the 09.47 train, Monday 22nd February. Geoff Cockshott asked once again whether anyone had seen Mr Lucas. Alan Carter, Judith Pearson, Ian Lavender and Sean Ashton said that they had not. Valerie Demeter said that she did not think she had seen any Mr Lucas either, but added that as she was driving to Marlborough on the morning in question at around ten, she *had* seen a scruffy man in his thirties carrying a rucksack, loitering suspiciously on the steps of the station and – so it seemed to her – bothering passers-by for change. Valerie Demeter said that she had reported the beggar to the police immediately. Half an hour later, PC Beresford telephoned and asked her to confirm her earlier description of the man, who had apparently now left the station and had been seen walking towards Chyde Community Centre.

Although Kenneth Renton was also unable to state with any confidence that he had seen Mr Lucas, he saw fit to interject at this point, for Valerie's account of the beggar at the station had, he said, solved something of a mystery for him. At 11.15 on that same morning, he had had to expel a gentleman from his weekly painting workshop. The gentleman in question had arrived late, adopting what Kenneth Renton could only describe as "a tone of dissembling cordiality" – as though he were not meeting the President of Chyde Art Club for the first time but rather renewing an acquaintance with an old friend. Though he did not know Kenneth Renton, he knew his name, which, as a seasoned confidence trickster, he had undoubtedly gleaned during the course of his research into Chyde and its environs; evidently, he thought Kenneth Renton's painting workshop an excellent place to begin exploiting the parish's manifold criminal opportunities. Kenneth Renton was equally cordial at first ("in the way that one instinctively is in cases of mistaken identity"), but soon gathered by the gentleman's manner that he had no intention of supplying the Associate Member Fee levied on all newcomers. Moreover, when asked to provide a utility bill bearing a local postcode, that he might be provisionally entered in the Associate Member Book (on the understanding that he bring the membership fee the following week), the gentleman was not only unable to provide such a document but incredulous that he should be required to do so. Under the circumstances, Kenneth Renton had had no choice but to ask him to leave. Kenneth Renton added that he dimly recalled the gentleman protesting – with an audacity typical of confidence tricksters – that he "thought that this had all been arranged", that he had "waited at the station for over half an hour..." Kenneth Renton interrupted that he had no idea what he was going on about and attempted to usher him towards the door. The gentleman became agitated; a scuffle ensued. At that moment, an officer of the law appeared and arrested the gentleman for disturbance of the peace. Kenneth Renton concluded that this was almost certainly the same gentleman who had been seen begging outside the station.

Geoff Cockshott deduced that if two people had seen this vagabond roaming the village, then they would surely also have seen Mr Lucas, had there *been* any Mr Lucas in the village at that time. Geoff Cockshott said he would get in touch with his friends in Chieveley to investigate what had happened to him. ACTION: GC.

5.2 The Chyde to Lexham Sponsored Bike Ride

The Chyde to Lexham Sponsored Bike Ride, organized by Michael Hewitt, raised £406. It was agreed that all monies would be placed in the Cricket Pavilion Rebuilding Fund.

5.3 Ian Lavender's "Fathers Afield" initiative

Ian Lavender was asked to give a report of his "Fathers Afield" initiative, aimed at finding ways for busy professional men – like himself, Ian Lavender – to spend more time with their children. Unlike Geoff Cockshott, Ian Lavender had not typed out his report, giving an off-the-cuff summary of February's trip to the New Forest. The gist of this brief report was that things had gone "quite well". When asked to supply further details, Ian Lavender replied that he did not particularly want to talk about it. Kenneth Renton stated that he was not satisfied with this, demanding to know how the VCC's limited budget was being spent.

At this point Ian Lavender stood up and announced that he had made an alarming discovery last weekend in the New Forest. Initially he talked fondly of the trip, recalling how much closer all the fathers had felt in this new context, not just to their own sons and daughters, but to the other fathers' children. He talked of how the hustle and bustle of the cramped youth hostel and its domestic regime had thrown them all together, how barriers had been broken down through the agency of communal work. However, Ian Lavender intimated that in certain quarters the intimacy had taken on a disquieting and ultimately monstrous aspect. Michael Hewitt, he said, had got particularly "involved" last weekend. Ian Lavender had welcomed this at first, believing it to be an overcompensation for the fact that, as driver of the bus, he had been starved of contact with the children for the three-hour journey. But according to Ian Lavender, Michael Hewitt hadn't "let up" for the entire weekend, even refusing to join the adults' Saturday-night trip to the pub in order to watch over the children. Michael Hewitt seemed, in Ian Lavender's opinion, to "prefer the society of children". Ian Lavender stated that when the fathers returned from the pub, evidently earlier than Michael Hewitt had expected, they found – or rather he, Ian Lavender, found (the other fathers having gone to bed) – that Michael Hewitt had "left his own dormitory and…" At this point Ian Lavender tailed off, appearing to be on the verge of tears, planting both hands on the table to support his shaking body in a gesture that seemed to foretell the worst possible news. Ian Lavender then apologized to the Committee for not being able to continue. Alan Carter intervened at this point and said it was OK, they all knew what he was trying to tell them: that Michael Hewitt had strayed too far "afield". ACTION: AC, VD, GC, JD, SA, KR (w/ pitchforks and megaphone).

5.4 Mrs Pearson's Cheese and Wine Party

Mrs Pearson's Cheese and Wine Party raised over £500 for the National Canine Defence League. The raffle was won by Jane Randall of 16, The Maltings, The

Street, Tippington. Judith Pearson agreed to deliver the prize – two tickets to see *Pavarotti in the Park* – on her way home.

6. Meeting dates for remainder of 1992

The following meeting dates were agreed:

15th April
12th May
9th June
14th July
3rd September
1st October
2nd November
5th December

7. Treasurer's Report

Geoff Cockshott said that before he delivered his Treasurer's Report he needed a piss. After he left the room the Committee expressed disappointment that the horse tranquilizers they had put in Geoff Cockshott's tea had had no noticeable effect. Kenneth Renton remarked that he seemed as inscrutable as ever. Valerie Demeter urged patience, suggesting that the uncharacteristic candour of Geoff Cockshott's announcement that he had to piss heralded imminent psychogenic meltdown. Alan Carter concurred, adding that Geoff Cockshott would ordinarily have deprecated the human need to urinate with a coy euphemism such as "spend a penny" or "point Percy at the porcelain".

6.1 Draft budget approved

Geoff Cockshott, trembling slightly as he perused the minutes to the VCC's previous meeting, asked for a show of hands on the budget proposal he had suggested in February. Geoff Cockshott counted and recounted these hands several times, somehow contriving to arrive at a number far greater than the total quantity of hands possessed by those present at the VCC Executive Committee Meeting. The proposal was duly ratified.

6.2 Protocol governing expenses accounts

Geoff Cockshott, sweating and looking about the room in a state of mounting anxiety, asked Committee Members to come up with alternatives to the current protocol governing expenses accounts. These, he added, unzipping his cardigan and loosening his tie, would be discussed in April's meeting.

6.3 Reserves in annual accounts

Before sliding beneath the table, Geoff Cockshott was able to confirm that, having reviewed the annual accounts and offset the figures against projected expenses, he was now in a position to give the green light for the new spending initiatives they had discussed in November of last year. Geoff Cockshott then lost consciousness. Alan Carter placed him in the recovery position.

7. Any other business

There was no other business.

– Chyde Vicious Companions Club Monthly Newsletter, April 1992

& George

We are walking round now as sad as can be.
— Gilbert & George, *The Nature of Our Looking*

In his brilliant book *Gilbert & George: A Portrait*, Daniel Farson describes George's reaction to an autograph-hunter who had accosted him at an airport. After a volley of mumbled pleasantries – "Extraordinary... How kind... Charming..." – George took the pen and wrote "& George", so that Gilbert could sign his own name when he had finished browsing in the departure-lounge shops. It's a seemingly innocuous anecdote, but one that has great resonance for my niece, who happens to possess an "incomplete" G&G autograph obtained at a South London Gallery opening in 1994. It reads: "   & George", George having promised that Gilbert would "fill in the gap on his return from the lavatory". But he never did, for at this point the actor Keith Allen appeared from nowhere brandishing a bottle of champagne. It seemed impolite for a stranger to gatecrash this private celebration, so my niece beat a stealthy retreat, clutching the unfinished autograph.

How poignant that autograph has become in light of Gilbert's recent passing: what an acute symbol of bereavement that ampersand is.

Gilbert and George's beginning, and subsequent rise to prominence in the early 1970s, was rooted in studied anachronism and controlled antipathy. At a time of monolithic self-expression they assumed an air of utter conformity. That effete Edwardian deportment can't have gone down well with their hirsute peers at St Martins School of Art – which was of course an excellent reason for adopting it. As the inscription appended to their 1970 work *The Nature of Our Looking* implies, as soon as they graduated from Sir Anthony Caro's Unofficial Course in Advanced Sculpture, Gilbert & George devoted their lives to the expression of monumental pathos.

Interpretations of this stance range from scorn to eulogy. It would be insensitive at this sad time to offer an academic survey of them all (it is insensitive to offer an "academic" survey of anything at any time), but I am with those who suspect that the reason G&G included themselves so consistently in their work was to dramatize their own sense of isolation. As anyone who ever sighted G&G in the street will tell you, they seemed never to look quite at home anywhere in the world, and seemed *least* at home in the garish midst of their own imagery – which was of course an excellent reason for including themselves in so many of their works. Their inscrutable presence provided a pictorial counterpoint to profane or volatile subject matter, seeming somehow to both defuse and inflame it. They seemed to appear *in* the work while washing their hands *of* it, as though above blame, the conduits of universal rather than personal profanity. Likewise, their opinions, often consciously out of step with societal consensus, seemed designed not so much to express a personal credo as reveal universal antagonisms. They seemed to believe not in their own opinions per se but in their *effect*. For example, when Margaret Thatcher was ousted from Number 10, G&G were unstinting in their admiration for her.

For G&G timing was important – though whether it is comic timing that we see in their work is debatable. They have always been funny, but whether we were laughing *with* or *at* them – and whether they cared – remains unclear. I suspect both prepositions are inaccurate; theirs was an epic rather than comic timing. For in any given situation it was as if they already knew how they were going to behave and what they were going to say: they had merely to decide when to say it. G&G's very existence seemed "rehearsed". As *Living Sculptures*, their impact on the everyday realm arguably matched, and often surpassed, their impact on the art world. Daniel Farson's book contains a memorable account of a 1971 visit to New York to perform *The Singing Sculptures*. The critic Carter Ratcliffe took G&G on a river cruise around Manhattan Island. His commentary on the prominent features of the skyline was met with a series of stock responses:

"That's the 52nd Street pier."
"Marvellous."

"Super."
"Would you like anything to drink?"
"How terribly kind."
"It's a nice day, isn't it?"
"Oh yes, absolutely splendid."

When I said that G&G's pathos was monumental I was being literal, for I meant nothing less than that it was set in stone, that it exchanged human spontaneity for a set of stage directions: *Enter... make knowingly bourgeois remark... Exeunt.* Farson continues:

> Carter said that G&G used conversational forms they had found ready-made in the lyrics of 'Underneath the Arches', yet had adopted no Duchampian condescension – their refusal to be ironic was militant. Describing the weather or the view as "absolutely splendid", they were as utterly earnest in their tenth as in their first use of the phrase. Gilbert & George did not so much converse as offer rigidity, impersonality, monumental representations of what proper conversation should be. They were talking as living sculptures ought to talk.

Since the 1960s many artists who have purported to "live their work" have done so with the attendant claim of "demystifying" art. If G&G lived their work, it was not in order to demystify art but in order to mystify life. The demystification of art is usually traced back to Duchamp's introduction of the commonplace object into the artistic realm. Through the simple expedient of always appearing in public together, dressing in immaculate suits, finishing each other's sentences, G&G seemed to invert this convention, importing their own personal weirdness into the quotidian realm, at a time when the opposite tendency – placing the quotidian in the exalted realm of art – was approaching its zenith. This inversion was canny, for art's appropriation of the quotidian was always doomed to end in anticlimax, culminating as it has in the pseudo-democratic social formalism that is sometimes described as "relational aesthetics" – whose anodyne interactivity is so often a smokescreen for an absence of genuine artistic character.

The only thing we should feel entitled to *demand* of an artwork – be it expressionist painting, confessional film-making or the dourest of institutional critique – is that it have character. The prevalence of so much characterless work today is the main reason why the death of Gilbert Proesch is the worst thing that could possibly happen to the art world. His passing demands two obituaries: one to lament the passing of a man, another to announce the end of an oeuvre. And what of George Passmore? Sometimes the bereaved seek solace in the distraction of work, but this is difficult when the deceased is not just a loved one but also the other half of a creative partnership. The shadow cast by such a death is long, stretching beyond the surviving partner's sadness at the loss of a friend into an evident foreclosure of his immediate career prospects. Let us admit that such deaths quickly engender vulgar speculation: Is it Wise for Ernie to continue without Eric? Does Dawn know enough French to get by *sans* Saunders? With the passing of an individual artist, there is no such "What next for *the other guy*?", just a dignified inquest into the significance of his work by that coiffed cultural coroner, Sir Melvyn Bragg.

— *The Jersey Herald*, 2004

Acknowledgements

I'd like to acknowledge the help and encouragement offered by the following people during the writing of this book: Barry Dobbin, Nigel Cooke, Caragh Thuring, Chris Jeffries, Tim Bailey, Rachel Reupke, Moyra Derby, Jaspar Joseph-Lester, Neil Rumming, Jordan Bass at McSweeney's, Matthew McDonald, David Dye, Lohan Immanuel, Matthew Arnatt, Tim White, Max Bruce, Rowan Cope, Richard Beales, Sally O'Reilly, Nicholas de Ville, Matthew Poole and Amanda Beech, who all read various bits of it in some shape or form despite having better things to do. I'd like to thank everyone at Alma Books for their meticulous work. Thanks especially to Alessandro Gallenzi and Elisabetta Minervini for their advice and great care in producing this book, to say nothing of their enthusiasm. I am indebted to the late K.C. Harrison's Introduction to the book *Public Library Buildings 1975–1983*, which served as a broad template for 'Public Brothels 1975–85'. I should also mention the artists featured here: Jamie Shovlin (and by association Mike Harte), Elizabeth Price, Tim Bailey, Gilbert & George and Wim Delvoye, all of whose work I respect greatly, despite my irreverent treatment of it. Thanks also to Brendan Fahy for allowing me to record his not-so-misspent youth for posterity. Above all, I am indebted to Pat O'Connor, without whose support I would have given up long ago.

ERRATA:

The first two lines of Ted Hughes's poem quoted on p. 156 have been erroneously inverted. The beginning of the poem should therefore read:

"A Nation's a soul. / A Soul is a Wheel"

The following credit should be added to the copyright page:

"Philip Larkin's poem on p. 155 and Ted Hughes's poem on p. 156 have been reproduced with kind permission of Faber and Faber Ltd."